KEEP ON MOVING!

Entrepreneurial Creativity and
Effective Problem Solving

21 MAY 04

Best Wishes

McGraw-Hill Higher Education

A Division of The McGraw-Hill Companies

Permissions and acknowledgements

The MIT story on page 1 is used with permission from the President's Office of MIT. It was originally published by *The Tech* (Vol. 111, No. 28, 6/26/91, page 2).

The graph on page 4 is used with permission by Gerald Udell, Southwest Missouri State University. The original appeared in *Evaluating Potential New Products: A Manual to Aid in Understanding the Innovation Process and the PIES-VIII Preliminary Innovation Evaluation System*, 1998.

Chapter 4 and Chapter 5 (except for the kitchen lighting example) have been condensed from material in *Creative Problem Solving and Engineering Design* by Edward Lumsdaine, Monika Lumsdaine, and J. William Shelnutt, © 1999 McGraw-Hill Primis, ISBN 0-07-236-058-5.

The Ned Herrmann materials (particularly in Chapter 3) are used by permission of Herrmann International, © 2002 by The Ned Herrmann Group, © 1998, 1986 by Ned Herrmann. We gratefully acknowledge the kindness of Herrmann International for generously permitting us to use copyrighted materials from their books and HBDI packets. For more information see: **www.hbdi.com**.

We thank Professor John Pliniussen (course developer) and Professor Peg Tittle (course instructor) for permission to use exercises (i.e., the "Don't sell me" game and "The problem at Algona") from the manual that accompanies the course ADMN 3917EQ *Innovation and Creativity* in the Centre for Continuing Business Education, Nipissing University, North Bay, Ontario, Canada.

Monika Lumsdaine, management consultant for corporate behavior of Hancock, Michigan, has done the major editing and initial word processing for the manuscript. She has been instrumental in integrating text written by two different authors into one synthesized whole. As certified HBDI evaluator, she has contributed to the text in Chapter 3 and originated the "wheel" maps in Part 2.

SPJ Marketing, Hutton Business Centre, Bridge Works, Bentley, Doncaster (UK) have developed the new artwork and produced the final page layout for the book. They are also the designers of the book's cover.

KEEP ON MOVING!
Entrepreneurial Creativity and Effective Problem Solving

3 4 5 6 7 8 9 0 QSR QSR 0 9 8 7 6 5 4 3

ISBN 0-07-284153-2

Printer/Binder: Quebecor World

KEEP ON MOVING!

Entrepreneurial Creativity and
Effective Problem Solving

Professor Edward Lumsdaine
Michigan Technological University

Professor Martin Binks
The University of Nottingham

ISBN 0-07-284153-2

Permissions and acknowledgments

The MIT story on page 1 is used with permission from the President's Office of MIT. It was originally published by *The Tech* (Vol. 111, No. 28, 6/26/91, page 2).

The graph on page 4 is used with permission by Gerald Udell, Southwest Missouri State University. The original appeared in *Evaluating Potential New Products: A Manual to Aid in Understanding the Innovation Process and the PIES-VIII Preliminary Innovation Evaluation System,* 1998.

Chapter 4 and Chapter 5 (except for the kitchen lighting example) have been condensed from material in Creative Problem Solving and Engineering Design by Edward Lumsdaine, Monika Lumsdaine, and J. William Shelnutt, ©1999 McGraw-Hill Primis, ISBN 0-07-236-058-5.

The Ned Herrmann materials (particularly in Chapter 3) are used by permission of Herrmann International, ©2002 by The Ned Herrmann Group, ©1998, 1986 by Ned Herrmann. We gratefully acknowledge the kindness of Herrmann International for generously permitting us to use copyrighted materials from their books and HBDI packets. For more information see: www.hbdi.com.

We thank Professor John Pliniussen (course developer) and Professor Peg Tittle (course instructor) for permission to use exercises (i.e., the "Don't sell me" game and "The problem at Algona") from the manual that accompanies the course *ADMN 3917EQ Innovation and Creativity* in the Centre for Continuing Business Education, Nipissing University, North Bay, Ontario, Canada.

Monika Lumsdaine, management consultant for corporate behavior of Hancock, Michigan, has done the major editing and initial word processing for the manuscript. She has been instrumental in integrating text written by two different authors into one synthesized whole. As certified HBDI evaluator, she has contributed to the text in Chapter 3 and originated the "wheel" maps in Part 2.

SPJ Marketing, Hutton Business Centre, Bridge Works, Bentley, Doncaster (UK) have developed the new artwork and produced the final page layout for the book. They are also the designers of the book's cover.

Table of Contents

List of Figures

List of Tables

List of Activities

Preface

Entrepreneurial creativity refers to the source of new ideas that can lead to economic development. Effective problem solving is about producing solutions. The combination of the two creates economic improvement for individuals, groups, communities and society through successful entrepreneurship.

Why should you read this book?

This book answers the questions of why, who, where, when, what and how of creative entrepreneurship and starting a business. It includes a discussion of the nature of entrepreneurship and of the underlying thinking skills required, together with a highly effective process for problem solving.

We have designed the book to be concise and accessible by focusing only on the content that our long experience of teaching in these areas has revealed to be most valuable for learners with a wide variety of backgrounds and requirements. This practical book will be useful for those interested in an introduction to entrepreneurship or in creativity or in effective problem solving or any combination thereof.

- Some readers may be considering a career in entrepreneurship; they will gain helpful insights as a result of learning more about the nature of entrepreneurship, the ways of encouraging creative thinking and the systematic steps of effective problem solving that are then applied to the entire process of starting a business.

- Others may be interested in improving their ability in a particular aspect of the coverage such as creative thinking or effective problem solving that can be applied across a wide range of needs and situations. Bringing these aspects together in a focus on entrepreneurship reflects the present upsurge in demand for the skills associated with entrepreneurial creativity and effective problem solving.

Why focus on creativity, effective problem solving and entrepreneurship?

Successful entrepreneurship is a complex activity requiring a combination of personal traits, competencies and abilities, some of which are innate, some of which are latent or dormant and some of which can be learned. Some successful entrepreneurs are "naturals," born out of their genetics and the experiences life has provided. But for many others, there is a growing appreciation of the need to enhance certain aspects of the entrepreneurial persona in order to improve their lives and achievements. Characteristics such as the ability to think and behave more creatively and to solve problems more effectively are helpful under most conditions.

In the broader context, economic development is generated through successful entrepreneurship. Appropriate political and social institutions, integrity and good judgment then support the efforts of individuals. Successful entrepreneurship includes the ability to respond to changing conditions in an effective and efficient manner. As the pace of change in terms of technology and social needs accelerates, the role of effective and successful entrepreneurship becomes more important. It is for this reason that we have chosen to link this book with successful entrepreneurial endeavor even though it addresses a far wider audience in terms of its more general relevance to developing creative thinking and problem solving skills. At the very least, the application to entrepreneurship makes a natural and interesting example and case study.

How is the book organized?

The content of the book is divided into two parts and ten chapters where each part has a different focus, purpose and learning requirements. Part 1 (in five chapters) provides a basic understanding of creativity, entrepreneurship and an effective problem-solving approach with specific tools that can be used at each step. Part 2 (in five chapters related to the five steps of creative problem solving) gives the practical application of the models and skills learned in Part 1. It is all about how to start a business "from idea to market" as a creative entrepreneur!

Chapter 1 addresses the question, "Why do you want to be an entrepreneur?" It helps potential entrepreneurs investigate their motivation, the personal context, and some of the decision making required for the successful launch of a new enterprise. It also presents an overview of how creative problem solving supports the steps in the development of a product.

Chapter 2 provides a foundational understanding of the nature of entrepreneurial creativity. It first looks at the historical context of entrepreneurship and its economic contribution—it considers definitions and theories of entrepreneurship in a summary starting with the work of Richard Cantillon 250 years ago to Joseph Schumpeter in the first half of the 20th century and Amar Bhidé at the threshold of a new century. A synthesis of past and present theories of creativity is followed by an exploration of its role in the entrepreneurial process. Then the focus shifts to individual creativity and how to enhance it. The chapter concludes with an examination of four factors required to increase innovation in an organization.

Chapter 3 presents the Herrmann model of brain dominance; it will provide an understanding of the different thinking skills required to be a successful entrepreneur. This model is a powerful tool for improving thinking, learning, communication and teamwork.

Chapter 4 introduces a structured approach for effective problem solving. Each step is associated with a particular metaphorical mindset involving specific thinking skills to achieve optimum results.

Chapter 5 discusses the principles of the Pugh method, a creative concept evaluation technique. The steps are illustrated with several examples, one of which is a case study with completed evaluation matrixes for three rounds.

Chapter 6 sees individual and societal problems not only as constraints upon economic development, but as sources for potential new ideas and entrepreneurial opportunities. Various tools, applications and benefits of using the explorer's mindset for finding a problem to solve are examined, including playing the "Don't sell me" game. Some useful web sites for "explorers" are identified and guidelines for the inventor's log are provided, as well as tips for focusing a problem. The detective's mindset is used to investigate the *real* problem and discover the *real* customers. Tips are provided for conducting a user needs survey.

Chapter 7 elaborates on some tools that can enhance the effectiveness of brainstorming and creative thinking. The topic of intellectual property protection, with a focus on patents, is discussed in some detail, with useful tips and links for entrepreneurs and inventors.

Chapter 8 provides additional details on the Pugh method evaluation process, including the concurrent analytical and assessment activities needed by entrepreneurs, such as market, cost, and risk analyses, to bring product development to the prototype stage.

Chapter 9 focuses on the decision-making process and documentation necessary for finding and developing a "best" solution. Much of this documentation will later feed into the preparation of a business plan. Sources for idea assessment are identified, and guidelines are provided for evaluating the profit potential of the new business. Other decisions to be made at this point relate to the legal format of the business and the development of a marketing plan.

Chapter 10 gives tips on how to make an effective presentation for selling ideas or inventions. The creative problem solving process is reviewed with attention on how to improve an entrepreneur's chances of success. How startup enterprises are financed is discussed, and some reasons for looking beyond startup are presented. Directions and resources are provided for writing a business plan, together with a checklist to be used immediately prior to business startup. The book closes by encouraging entrepreneurs (and all readers) to develop a habit of periodically reviewing what has been learned— from success as well as failure which can then be used as a stepping stone to "keep on moving" forward.

Each chapter in Part 1 aims to transmit factual knowledge and the foundational principles, together with hands-on activities or exercises and opportunities for application and further learning in order to provide a basic understanding of creativity and entrepreneurship. Part 2 focuses on the practical aspects of how to be a creative entrepreneur and start a business, while at the same time illustrating the iterative application of effective problem solving. We tried to provide the most up-to-date information as of time of printing (August 2002). However, web sites especially can change at a very rapid pace. If a particular source or reference is no longer available, you may be able to access similar information via a search engine such as **www.google.com**.

This book provides two types of learning opportunities: explicit and tacit. You, the reader, will learn information or explicit conceptual knowledge *about* a topic and will then have the opportunity to acquire tacit operational knowledge *by doing* a task, exercise, or application in a particular thinking mode. We believe that this book is unique in that the underlying thinking skills needed in the creative problem solving process and its application to launching a successful business are purposefully made transparent. This helps people be more effective in applying what they are learning from this book to their jobs, their enterprises, and their personal lives.

TIPS TO ENHANCE LEARNING

➤ *Underline or highlight important ideas and concepts as you read.*
➤ *Jot down questions and conmments that come to mind as you read.*
➤ *Do the activities and exercises in Part 1 of the text.*

Who are the authors?

Dr. Edward Lumsdaine is currently Professor of Mechanical Engineering at Michigan Technological University and Management Consultant for Ford Motor Company. He also holds an appointment as Special Professor of Business in the Institute for Enterprise and Innovation at the University of Nottingham (England). In 1994 he received the America Society for Engineer Education (ASEE) Chester F. Carlson award for innovation in engineering education. He has co-authored books and teaches workshops in creative problem solving, entrepreneurship and innovation—a synthesis of many years of experience as engineer in industry as well as dean of engineering and professor at six different universities in the US and four different universities abroad. Professor Lumsdaine is a Fellow of ASME (American Society of Mechanical Engineering) and the Royal Society of Arts (RSA). His engineering specialties are in aeroacoustics, vibration, heat transfer, fluid mechanics, and energy conservation, and he has published over 100 papers in these fields. Several times, Professor Lumsdaine and Professor Binks have jointly taught a course in entrepreneurship and effective problem solving for MBA students in Singapore and Malaysia—this book has grown out of this cooperative effort.

Dr. Martin Binks is the Director of the Institute for Enterprise and Innovation at the University of Nottingham (UNIEI) and Professor of Entrepreneurial Development at the University, specializing in entrepreneurship and the financing of small and medium enterprises (SMEs), with an established research background in the area of SMEs and their relationship with banks. Among his activities and accomplishments are visiting professor to the Claremont Graduate School in California; provision of consultancy to HM Government ministries and member of the Bank of England Governor's Seminar on the Financing of Small Firms; council member of the Small Business Research Trust; and Associate Editor of *The Journal of Small Business Finance*. Professor Binks developed one of the first university-level courses in entrepreneurship in the UK. His research focus is in three areas: entrepreneurship, SME finance, and the development of internet-based survey procedures such as the United Kingdom Business Barometer (www.ukbb.ac). Professor Binks is a Fellow of the Royal Society of Arts (RSA).

PART 1

Understanding Creativity and Entrepreneurship

Chapter 1
Personal Motivation

"Keep on Moving!" — How can this benefit me?

Charles Vest, President of MIT (Massachusetts Institute of Technology), has told the following true story in his commencement addresses at MIT in 1991 and 1998:

> Some years ago, an MIT alumnus came up to our former president, Jerry Wiesner and said, "Dr. Wiesner, do you remember me? You shook my hand as I came through the line at my graduation twenty years ago ... and you told me something that changed my entire life. It was the secret of my successful career." Jerry reluctantly admitted that he could not remember the moment and asked, "What did I say?" With great emotion, the alumnus answered, "President Wiesner, you said, 'Keep on moving ... keep on moving.'"

This book will help you to keep on moving, no matter who you are or at what stage of life you find yourself in at the moment—because we live in rapidly changing times. You will be prepared to recognize and use and profit from the opportunities (expected or unexpected) that will come your way. Although the book is written in the context of entrepreneurship, the principles can be applied by anyone in many different contexts and situations, because an entrepreneurial mindset will help you cope with change.

> **Even if you are on the right track, you'll get run over if you just sit there.**
> Will Rogers

This chapter explores the question of what it takes to be a creative entrepreneur by looking at the *why*—your motivation. The benefits of learning effective problem solving skills are also presented. The *who*, *what* and *how* of understanding the entrepreneurship models and thinking skills are addressed in detail in the remaining chapters of Part 1. Then the *what*, *when*, *where* and *how* of starting a creative enterprise are given in Part 2 of this book in iterative "wheels" that move through a structured sequence of different thinking modes and problem-solving mindsets.

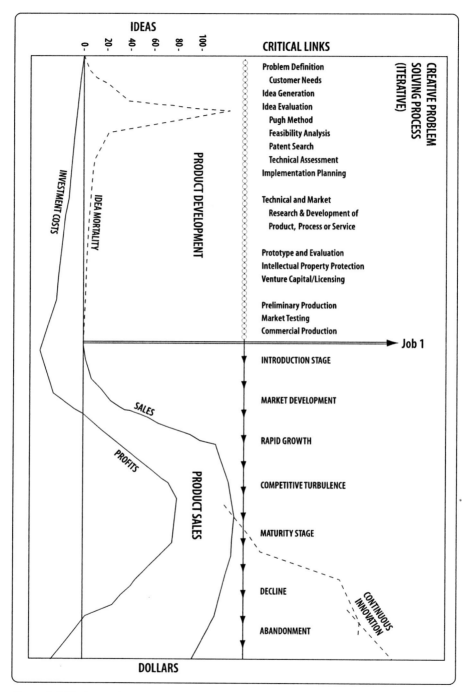

Figure 1.1 *The innovation process in the life cycle of a product (adapted from a graph by Gerald Udell [Ref. 1.1])*

Why do we need effective problem solving and entrepreneurial skills?

Having effective problem solving skills benefits you personally, but the benefits extend to your organization or business and to society. Personally, you are better able to cope with change; you develop more effective thinking, learning, communication and teamwork skills—all of which lead to a more enjoyable life. Professionally, you are able to solve problems and make decisions more effectively, and you are able to create an invigorating work environment leading to a successful career. In your business or organization, you are able to provide a product or service that meets the needs of the customer; you are able to guide or lead the direction of technological development and innovation leading to increased productivity, and you are able to gain and maintain a competitive position in the global marketplace. Societal benefits are new ideas for solving ecological, technical, economic and social problems. Effective problem solving is the foundation for developing ideas and then selecting the best idea for starting and continuing a successful business, as shown in Figure 1.1 on the facing page.

This book concentrates on providing skills and information for the product development phase. Then, through the application of continuous innovation, new products can be developed to maintain the profitability of our enterprises. But if we stand still and fail to innovate, we will fall behind our competition. None of the critical links in the product development and effective problem solving process should be skipped or undertaken out of sequence if we want to obtain optimal results.

The ability for generating new ideas is important. According to Charles Stanley, Vice President of Motorola, "Large companies in the future will rely heavily on small companies to bring innovation, through licensing or acquisition." In our rapidly changing high tech information age, communication of knowledge and information in teams and networks has become essential. In addition to *what* and *how*, entrepreneurial thinking skills, continuous learning and understanding *why* have become crucial for everyone. Table 1.1 compares key issues in the old and new economy—entrepreneurial organizational forms now have an important contribution to make in the new economic paradigm.

What is the impact of entrepreneurship education? To find out, the Eller College of Business at the University of Arizona compared MBA alumni who graduated from their entrepreneurship program with alumni from the traditional business program.

Table 1.1 *A New Economic Paradigm*

ISSUE	OLD ECONOMY	NEW ECONOMY
Markets	Stable	Dynamic
Scope of competition	Regional/national	Global
Organizational form	Hierarchical	Networked, entrepreneurial
Mobility of business	Low	High
Key factors of production	Capital + labor	Knowledge + innovation
Effect of innovation	Moderate	High
Institutional/firm relations	Self-sufficient	Alliances and collaboration
Business – government relations	Impose requirements	Assist firms; deregulation
Leading research areas	Physical sciences and disciplinary engineering	Information systems & biological sciences

The study discovered that entrepreneurship graduates reaped the following benefits:

- Three times more likely to start a new business.
- Three times more likely to be self employed; less likely to work for government.
- Earning annual incomes that are 27% higher and owning 62% more assets.
- In large corporations, earning about $23,000/year more than their counterparts.
- More satisfied with their jobs.
- Dramatically increasing sales growth in small firms (by 900%).
- Working for high tech firms in greater numbers.
- More involved in product development and R&D activities.

When ingenious, creative thoughts result in a new product or process, we have an invention. When the invention is adopted widely through entrepreneurial activity and results in permanent change, we can say that innovation has occurred (see page 25 for further discussion). However, the great majority of inventions never reach the marketplace. Accurate figures are impossible to come by, but one survey by NESTA in the UK suggests that the odds stack up something like this:

- Only 1 in 100 inventions more than covers its costs.
- Only 1 in 300 inventions makes a significant difference to a company.
- Only 1 in 1400 inventions is a world-beater leading to innovation.

This looks like an abysmal failure rate, but it need not be. Most failures are either inevitable because of flaws in the idea, or they are made inevitable by the inventor's mishandling of some aspect of development. Inventors who focus on avoiding mistakes can vastly increase the odds of succeeding, and this is what this book is all about.

Why do you want to be an entrepreneur?

Do you, like most people, want to be an entrepreneur because you want to be your own boss—you want freedom from the 9 to 5 work routine? Are autonomy and independence the main attractions for you? The greater the respect you have for your own judgment, the less you have for that of others. This may present problems, because as an employee, you could be a constant source of disagreement and distraction in your workplace. At the same time, you may feel very frustrated and angry, and the strong negative feelings prevent you from recognizing positive opportunities. If you are in this position, running your own business as an entrepreneur may be a better choice.

There are other good reasons for wanting to be an entrepreneur. Do you want to make money? Are you bored by your existing job? Do you want to be more creative and to more fully use your skills and knowledge? Or have you been made redundant—has your job disappeared? Do you have an idea that just won't go away and are you convinced there is a demand for this product or service? What do others say you are good at? Take time to write down *your* motives, technical qualifications and marketable interests!

Have you considered some of the difficulties you may face? Running a business often requires extended hours (up to 16 hours, six or seven days a week), especially during startup. Do you have the emotional and physical stamina, as well as the time to run a business? What will be the effect on your family? Is your family supportive? Are you a self-starter or a procrastinator; do you have self-discipline and will power? How good are your creative ideas and your decisions? Do you enjoy competition? How well are you able to get along with all kinds of people? Do you have planning, managerial, and organizational skills? The adage "If you fail to plan, you plan to fail" applies particularly to entrepreneurs. Are you able to tolerate calculated risk? Can you face losing your life savings? Are you prepared to get the necessary business training, resources and skills before plunging into your business venture? How well do you know yourself? Jot down weaknesses and perceived problem areas where you will need to pay particular attention—you may gain valuable insight as you read through this book and apply what you are learning.

> *Throughout the entrepreneurship process, take every opportunity to sell yourself, your team, and your idea. You can never predict the benefits that such salesmanship will gain for you down the road.*
> NCIIA

Who should be an entrepreneur?

If you know yourself, if you know your product, and if you know your customer, you need not fear failure—you can increase the odds for success. Chapter 3 will provide much insight about the thinking skills you may need to develop to deal with potential pitfalls. Part 2 will guide you in how to develop a business idea into a marketable product or service. But first, you may find it fun as well as instructional to take the following quiz provided by the US Government Small Business Administration (SBA).

QUIZ FOR SMALL BUSINESS SUCCESS
(from Ref. 1.2)

We at *Small Business Success Magazine* conducted a survey of more than 100 California business owners. Their comments about small business success guided us in creating the following quiz. Choose the one answer you think (or feel) is best for each question and circle the corresponding letter, starting on the next page. Use the scorebox at the end of the quiz to determine your total point score and success quotient. There are no wrong answers. Each answer listed represents a segment of the responses we had to questions in the survey—the final rankings correspond with the importance successful owners gave to different answers.

1. **What is the key to business success?**
   a. business knowledge
   b. market
   c. hands-on management
   d. sufficient capital
   e. hard work

2. **If a relative ever asks for advice about starting a business I will tell them to**
   a. work for someone else in the field first
   b. write a business plan
   c. study marketing
   d. give up the idea
   e. learn about budgeting

3. **Which is the largest potential trouble spot?**
   a. too much growth
   b. too little growth
   c. too fast growth
   d. too slow growth
   e. sporadic growth

4. **I trust (select as many as apply)**
   a. nobody
   b. myself
   c. my partner
   d. a few key employees
   e. my customers

5. **I am unhappy when my employees are**
   a. late
   b. unhappy
   c. abrupt with customers
   d. resigning
   e. less dedicated than me

6. **My customers are (select as many as apply)**
   a. always right
   b. too fussy
   c. demanding
   d. worth listening to
   e. dumb

7. **Rank these in order of importance for small business success**
   a. word-of-mouth
   b. advertising
   c. signs
   d. location
   e. community events

8. **When it comes to money, I am**
   a. careful
   b. too carefree
   c. emotional
   d. shrewd
   e. hard nosed

9. **Financially my firm**
   a. has trouble with cash flow
   b. has a good line of credit
   c. is financed totally by receipt —no credit
   d. is making better profits this year than last year
   e. knows exactly where it is, always

10. **In hiring people**
    a. I take far too long
    b. I look for the cheapest person
    c. personality is more important than experience
    d. I look for the best person and I am willing to pay
    e. I only hire at the trainee level

11. **With my employees**
   a. I treat everybody the same
   b. I try to talk privately to everybody weekly
   c. as much as possible I tailor assignments to personalities
   d. I encourage them to talk to me about the business
   e. I try & work alongside them if possible

13. **Competition is**
   a. dumb
   b. smart
   c. cunning
   d. everywhere
   e. a constant threat

15. **I keep**
   a. careful financial records
   b. in touch with my customers
   c. in touch with my employees
   d. trying new techniques
   e. wanting to retire

17. **I think business plans are**
   a. for the birds
   b. nice but not necessary
   c. something I can do with my accountant
   d. useful and informative
   e. essential—I wouldn't do business without one

19. **What does a business need most?**
   a. money
   b. market research
   c. help
   d. time
   e. a solid business plan

12. **The real key to business success is**
   a. hard work and perseverance
   b. fine products and service
   c. knowing the fundamentals of business
   d. advertising
   e. employees

14. **The best competitive advantage is**
   a. experience
   b. understanding what the market wants
   c. confidence
   d. conducting a business ethically
   e. a detailed plan

16. **My dream is**
   a. to grow the business until someone else can run it
   b. to work until I drop
   c. to give up these headaches and have more fun at work
   d. to try another business
   e. to take a vacation

18. **What makes a terrific entrepreneur?**
   a. creativity
   b. discipline
   c. consumer orientation
   d. technical proficiency
   e. flexibility

20. **What is essential to marketing?**
   a. a "sixth sense"
   b. market research
   c. customer awareness
   d. experience
   e. testing

Scoring

Find each question in the following scorebox. Write the score for the answer you selected in the margin next to every question. If you did not select the highest scoring choice, take a look at that one and try to figure out why it scored so well. When you have worked through the entire quiz, go back and add up your points. Then compare your total with the quotient range of some of California's most successful business people.

Scorebox

Question	Points					Score
1.	a = 5	b = 4	c = 3	d = 2	e = 1	_____
2.	a = 5	e = 4	b = 3	c = 2	d = 1	_____
3.	c = 5	a = 4	b = 3	d = 2	e = 1	_____
4.	b = 5	e = 4	d = 3	c = 2	a = 1	_____
5.	b = 5	d = 4	c = 3	a = 2	e = 1	_____
6.	d = 5	c = 4	a = 3	b = 2	e = 1	_____
7.	a = 5	d = 4	c = 3	b = 2	e = 1	_____
8.	a = 5	d = 4	e = 3	b = 2	c = 1	_____
9.	e = 5	d = 4	b = 3	a = 2	c = 1	_____
10.	d = 5	a = 4	c = 3	b = 2	e = 1	_____
11.	c = 5	d = 4	e = 3	b = 2	a = 1	_____
12.	e = 5	d = 4	a = 3	b = 2	c = 1	_____
13.	e = 5	d = 4	c = 3	b = 2	a = 1	_____
14.	a = 5	b = 4	c = 3	e = 2	d = 1	_____
15.	b = 5	a = 4	c = 3	d = 2	e = 1	_____
16.	e = 5	a = 4	b = 3	c = 2	d = 1	_____
17.	e = 5	d = 4	c = 3	b = 2	a = 1	_____
18.	c = 5	a = 4	b = 3	e = 2	d = 1	_____
19.	b = 5	e = 4	a = 3	d = 2	c = 1	_____
20.	c = 5	b = 4	e = 3	d = 2	a = 1	_____

Total Score = _____

Success Quotient

75–100 You are a successful entrepreneur whose operations reflect tried and true business practices.

50–74 Your business is probably headed for long-term success. But success will come sooner if you sharpen your awareness of solid management skills and marketing techniques.

25–49 While you may be enjoying customer loyalty and repeat business, never forget the savvy competition is always looking for ways to take the lead. Don't let comfort lull you into false security. Be creatively assertive!

0–24 You may well have the right product. But to sell it successfully, you need to increase your market awareness and improve your operating philosophy. Reach out for practical classes, seminars and advice from people who have good business track records. And—keep persevering. It's the key ingredient to success.

END OF QUIZ

What are some characteristics of young entrepreneurs?

Especially if you are young (let's say in your teens or early twenties), you may not have obtained a high score in the *Quiz for Small Business Success*, perhaps because in your past experience you never had to think about the kinds of questions asked in the quiz. An article on encouraging youthful enterprise published in the RSA Journal (Ref. 1.5) points out:

> *"Every week, around 550 businesses are started [in the UK] by young people aged under 25, and the failure rate amongst this age group is particularly high. There have been few studies to understand the specific needs and aspirations of young people going into business on their own, and many misconceptions have been propagated which fail to grasp young entrepreneurs' true characteristics."*

The author, Gerard Darby, in a year-long research project, has examined the background, behaviors, motivations and qualities of successful young entrepreneurs and has found the following key findings:

- Young entrepreneurs often show an inclination for enterprise at an early age, even when the surrounding culture is non-supportive.

- The main source of encouragement for young entrepreneurs comes from other entrepreneurs (including family members who run their own businesses).

- The media by and large have ignored the success of young entrepreneurs and the role models they could be for young people.

- Young people are also entrepreneurial in financing their fledging businesses, commonly working without compensation for a year or more and using many sources (in small amounts) to get started.

- Young entrepreneurs are characterized by drive, energy, and extraordinary resourcefulness—making up for the lack of experience. Other traits are listed in Table 1.2 and involve to a large degree right-brain thinking preferences (as seen in Chapter 3 in this book).

- Young entrepreneurs offer work opportunities that attract other like-minded and talented individuals.

Table 1.2 *Key Characteristics of Young Entrepreneurs (from Ref. 1.5)*

✓ A sense of integrity, where employees, customers and investors are treated as valuable partners in the business.

✓ Applying common sense to business.

✓ An extraordinary sense of what makes a good innovation in a product or service, and the resilience and resourcefulness to turn this into reality.

✓ A sense of humour (which is seen in their working environments, marketing and personality).

✓ Motivated by the challenge of creating something and being in control of their own destiny, not by the desire of large profits.

✓ Taking a long-term view of the development of their enterprise.

Among major obstacles faced by young entrepreneurs in the UK (and elsewhere) is the lack of education in entrepreneurial skills in the public school systems—skills that would benefit everyone. Also, "entrepreneurship would be better fostered if ... entrepreneurial endeavor were celebrated and failure recognized as often being a necessary component of success" (Ref. 1.5). This book aims to fill these gaps by teaching entrepreneurial thinking skills and providing "how-to" resources.

References and resources

1.1   Gerald Udell, *Evaluating Potential New Products: A Manual to Aid in Understanding the Innovation Process and the PIES-VIII Preliminary Innovation Evaluation System*, Southwest Missouri State University, 1998, p.4.

1.2   To access the quiz on-line, go to **www.sba.gov**. In the left-hand menu, click on the top button "Starting Your Business." In the menu that appears, click on the third button from the top: "Success Stories." In the list on SOME IDEAS ON HOW TO BE SUCCESSFUL, scroll past the stories and series to the quiz. You may want to explore the other two topics as well!

1.3   Joel Barker, *The New Business of Paradigms* videotape (classic edition, 26 minutes; 21ˢᵗ century edition: 18 minutes). For information see the web site **www.starthrower.com**. These new releases are excellent motivators on the issues of change and innovation. See also *Future Edge: Discovering the New Paradigms of Success*, Morrow, New York, 1992.

1.4   The National Endowment for Science, Technology and the Arts (NESTA) in Great Britain has an inventor's handbook with much useful information for British entrepreneurs. It can be found by clicking on "guidance and application" at **www.nesta.org.uk**.

1.5   Gerard Darby, "Encouraging Youthful Enterprise," RSA Journal, 1/6/2002, pp. 28-29. The report can be seen at **www.rsa.org.uk/onians**.

Action checklist

➤   If you want to go beyond annotating this book in the margins as you read, obtain a notebook for jotting down thoughts and ideas. It will become a valuable resource for future reference and enhance your learning.

➤   In the lines provided here (or in your notebook) write down your main motivation of why you want to study this book:

➤   As you finish reading each chapter, briefly review the material:
   (a) What are the most important concepts you have learned?—This will fix them in your memory since subsequent chapters will build on this foundation.
   (b) What are the most important questions you still have?—This will prime your mind to recognize the answers as you discover them in subsequent chapters or from other resources.

Chapter 2
Entrepreneurship and Creativity

This chapter explores the historical context of entrepreneurship and its economic contribution and then focuses on individual creativity, how it fits in the process of business development and how it is influenced by the organizational climate. The relationships between entrepreneurship, invention and innovation are examined. Exercises provide opportunities to practice and enhance creative and innovative thinking.

The historical context of entrepreneurship

To understand why the creative problem-solving model used in this book is effective, let us explore briefly some key historical routes in terms of entrepreneurship and creativity.

Activity 2.1: Defining Entrepreneurship

Before we consider the various definitions of entrepreneurship that have evolved over the years, take a moment to jot down some of the key characteristics which come to mind when thinking about entrepreneurs and entrepreneurship. This encourages an easy focus on the subject area. Share your thoughts with one or two other people. Did their views provide a broader picture as well as reveal stereotypes that are often associated with the terms? After you have studied this chapter, compare your initial definition with what you have learned.

_____

_____

_____

_____

_____

_____

_____

_____

_____

_____

When attempting to define entrepreneurs and entrepreneurship, we need to choose an appropriate point of focus. Entrepreneurs are people with particular characteristics and traits of behavior whereas entrepreneurship is the result of what entrepreneurs do and refers to events and their economic impact. Our concern in this book is mainly with individuals and the development of their entrepreneurial skills and capabilities. Such development is generally regarded as highly positive in its impact on individual effectiveness and, in turn, on society in general. We want to briefly examine how economists in the last 250 years have defined entrepreneurs.

Richard Cantillon (168? – 1734)

The first recorded use of the term entrepreneurship in an economic context was by Richard Cantillon in his *Essai Sur La Nature de Commerce en General*. In this essay first published in 1755, twenty-one years after his death, Cantillon uses the term entrepreneur many times to refer to individuals who pursue the profits from buying at a lower price than they expect to sell under conditions of uncertainty. In the case of a farmer as entrepreneur, the uncertainty arises because the farmer knows how much the input costs are to grow the crops but won't know what the market price will be when the harvest is gathered and taken to market.

The individuals first introduced by Cantillon are not necessarily innovative; they simply organize the means of production under conditions of uncertainty and, therefore, are involved in risk taking. In one sense, Cantillon was concerned with establishing a specific category of individual who organized the means of production and received an income in the form of entrepreneurial profit. He clearly perceived a need to differentiate this individual from those who constituted the labor input in the production process. Cantillon may have been referring in part to his own role since he was a banker and also a speculator for whom risk-taking was the norm. As a speculator and also as an individual, Cantillon made many enemies. One was the servant whom he sacked in 1734 and who returned a few days later to murder him!

Cantillon's view may fit many people's perception of an entrepreneur, but since we want to focus upon the essential role of entrepreneurial creativity, we will look in more detail at the attributes of entrepreneurs and the way they behave as they start up and conduct their enterprises. Some of the earliest observations on entrepreneurial characteristics were made by the great economist and entrepreneur Jean Baptiste Say.

Jean Baptiste Say (1767-1832)

Say is well known as a popularizer of the works of Adam Smith (1723-1790) who is often regarded as the father of economics. Say attributed Britain's success as a growing industrial nation to the "wonderful practical skills of her entrepreneurs" and gave these definitions (from H.G.J. Aitken, "The future of entrepreneurial research" in *Explorations in Entrepreneurial History*, 1963, 2ⁿᵈ series 1(1), pp. 3-9):

> [The entrepreneur is an economic agent who] unites all means of production—the labor of the one, the capital or the land of others and who finds in the value of the products which result from their employment the reconstitution of the entire capital that he utilizes, and the value of wages, the interest, and the rent which he pays, as well as the profits belonging to himself.

> The entrepreneur has judgment, perseverance and knowledge of the world as well as of business. He is called upon to estimate with tolerable accuracy the importance of the specific product, the probable amount of the demand and the means of its production. At one time, he must employ a great number of hands; at another, buy or order the raw material, collect laborers, find consumers, and give at all times a rigid attention to order and economy—in a word, he must possess the art of superintendence and administration. In the course of such complex operations, there are an abundance of obstacles to be surmounted, of anxieties to be repressed, of misfortunes to be repaired and of expedience to be devised.

Say is much more explicit than Cantillon about the individual characteristics of entrepreneurs. He emphasizes the multiplicity of roles that entrepreneurs must adopt successfully if they are to make profits, beyond merely organizing and paying for all inputs and selling the output at a higher price. Entrepreneurs are not simply concerned with the production process or the product market; they must also be able to deal successfully with financial markets and the markets for raw materials, production plant and equipment, as well as labor and premises. They must also be aware of relevant legislation as it applies in their area of activity and taxation. Inadequate skills or knowledge in any of these areas will lead to inefficiency and possibly failure. Say's entrepreneurs have problem-solving abilities to overcome all the challenges and unanticipated problems that confront them. Aside from the slightly unusual English and the absurd assumption that entrepreneurs are necessarily male, it is remarkable how well Say's observations apply in the modern world. But one explicit element is still missing, and that is entrepreneurial creativity—in Say's entrepreneurs, there is still nothing uniquely different, new or innovative about what they produce.

Joseph Schumpeter (1883-1950)

The element of difference, uniqueness, innovation and change that is missing from many perceptions of entrepreneurship is the central feature of entrepreneurs as depicted by Joseph Schumpeter. Despite the awkward translation from the original German, the boxed quote below conveys the essence of Schumpeter's view. When we are in the process of combining the factors of production—people, plant and equipment, raw materials, finance and premises—in a new way to generate a new product or process, then we can be called entrepreneurial. But as soon as this combination becomes established as a business and

> *Whatever the type, everyone is an entrepreneur only when he actually carries out new combinations, and loses that character as soon as he has built up his business.*
>
> Joseph Schumpeter

the newness and uniqueness are gone, the term no longer applies. It is an extreme position in insisting that only hitherto unknown concepts and ideas are entrepreneurial and this only as they emerge; once they are known and understood, they become part of the status quo and cease to be considered entrepreneurial.

Harvey Leibenstein (1922-1994)

Harvey Leibenstein (while teaching at Harvard University) put an alternative view of the role of entrepreneurship forward in 1976 in his book *Beyond Economic Man*. He reiterates Say's emphasis upon the coordination of many inputs in order to produce output, and he refers to

> *Entrepreneurs create or carry on an enterprise where not all markets are clearly defined and where relevant parts of the production function are not completely known.*
>
> Harvey Leibenstein

the input completion role of entrepreneurs. Leibenstein's definition is also useful for his focus upon what he termed "gap-filling" or the ability to spot opportunities in the market earlier than others and thus make profits by filling these gaps.

The main elements of the debate

The differences in opinion reflected in the preceding discussion demonstrate the confusion that surrounds the expression *entrepreneurship* and *entrepreneur*. The debate revolves around three main claims:

1. *Any risk taker or businessperson is an entrepreneur.* The problem with this definition is that it is too general and fails entirely to discriminate between

entrepreneurs who administer traditional economic processes and those who are the agents of change.

2. ***Entrepreneurs are reactive.*** They are associated with change in that they facilitate it in response to the perception of market gaps. Although they are associated with change, they do not cause it but merely enable it—they observe and seize opportunities rather than create them.

3. ***Entrepreneurs cause change and through it economic development.*** They are associated with significant changes in economic processes and products and are only entrepreneurial whilst they are undertaking these changes, ceasing to be so when the changes have become established. The problem with this view is that it is highly restrictive. Here, entrepreneurs will constitute only a tiny proportion of people running businesses.

To achieve a workable and useful synthesis of these differing views, it is necessary to refer briefly to three theoretical positions as well as recent research data compiled by Amar Bhidé in order to generate a framework that emphasizes the role of entrepreneurial creativity in economic development.

Joseph Schumpeter's theory of economic development

The crucial contribution made by Joseph Schumpeter in his book *The Theory of Economic Development* was to highlight the role of the entrepreneur as the catalyst for economic development. This contribution connects entrepreneurship, creativity and economic development. To understand the actual and potential impact of entrepreneurship, it is important to consider his analysis.

Schumpeter portrayed any economy as a collection of enterprises and businesses where each represented a particular combination of factors of production in the form of people, machines, land, premises, finance, and so on. In some sense every business relied for its market upon the successful activities of all the others. This interdependence through customer demand meant that changes in the nature or level of economic activity would be caused only when a new combination of factors of production was introduced.

The nature of changes as it affected Schumpeter's economy could be either gradual or discrete. Gradual change would do little to alter the nature of economic activity but would simply refer, for example, to alterations in design, new fashions and new ways of presentation. Discrete change represents a more fundamental step change in activity. Schumpeter defined this as a change in product or process that could not be traced back to the previous version in gradual, continuous steps.

A good example that distinguishes clearly between gradual and discrete change is the movement from long-playing (LP) music recordings to compact discs (CD). The most recent LP record deck can be traced back through gradual steps to the original vertical wax cylinder, needle and sound cone or horn from which it was derived. The CD represents a complete break in the technology of sound reproduction, with no clear technological path backwards to the LP. Similar observations can be applied to many technological developments and the economic progress these innovations created.

Discrete change and lateral thinking

The importance of Schumpeter's perception of entrepreneurship is the similarity to what has been labeled *lateral thinking* or *thinking out of the box*. Lateral thinking depends on the ability to make associations that are in some senses illogical since they do not result from a clear linear thinking process where the connections are obvious. Let us illustrate with an example—calculating the number of matches in a singles knockout tennis competition. Given the number of entrants, let us assume 268, the linear thinker will start to calculate the number of matches in each round that will eventually lead to a single champion. The lateral approach to this question would start with the number of losers and would simply observe that 267 must equal the number of games played since each player can only lose once. Methods are available for encouraging a more lateral approach to thinking, particularly when confronted with specific problems. Indeed much of the rest of this book is dedicated to processes for achieving precisely this end. The important point here is the clear association between Schumpeterian entrepreneurship, lateral thinking and economic development.

Schumpeter also points out that significant resistance to entrepreneurship may often occur since by definition entrepreneurship involves the unfamiliar. For example, there may be social resistance to a new medical technique. Institutional resistance may be encountered in the financial institutions considering applications for funding or in businesses where a new technology requires replacement of equipment that has been rendered obsolete yet may be quite new with years of productive life remaining. The successful entrepreneur is therefore the individual who breaks down the logjam of resistance and enables a wave of innovation or paradigm shifts to occur that will often cause the replacement of an existing technology with a new one. Schumpeter described this process as one of "creative destruction" that captures brilliantly the notion of dynamic progress and development as opposed to moribund stagnation. The depiction of economic development as the end result of applied creativity through innovation has enormous significance because it implies that an effective increase in applied creativity will cause acceleration in economic development.

However, this particular view of entrepreneurship is highly restrictive in that it only accepts discrete (or catalytic) change as entrepreneurship. To capture the full significance of entrepreneurship it is also necessary to consider two other viewpoints alongside the dramatic catalytic impact described by Schumpeter.

The elusive equilibrium—an Austrian view

The Austrian school of economics sees economies as dynamic and ever changing, never still. Casual observation suggests that this scene of perpetual disequilibria is an accurate portrayal of economies in practice. Process and outputs are changing; resources are employed in different ways, and external shocks change trading conditions. Much of this volatility is a result of changes in the underlying conditions of demand and supply. Demand for goods and services depend on tastes and consumer preferences, and these vary through time. Supply conditions change as new technology arises, creating new production possibilities. Prices and outputs do not move randomly, however; they reflect the economic adjustment to new conditions in demand or supply or both.

According to the Austrian school, entrepreneurs play a crucial role in this dynamic process. Changes to demand or supply create the potential for profit. The first people to notice and respond to an increase in demand for a particular product or service will be able to charge higher prices while costs remain unchanged. When others enter the marketplace to satisfy the increase in demand, the resulting competition may spur some of the pioneers to look for new profit opportunities created by new imbalances in demand and supply in other markets.

Thus entrepreneurs and their alertness to opportunities for profit ensure that resources in the economy are constantly reallocated in line with the changing patterns of supply and demand. Without their alertness and quick responsiveness, imbalances in markets would occur, with shortages in some areas and surpluses in others.

Although the economy never reaches a stable state of equilibrium, in a sense entrepreneurial activity is forever pursuing and tracking that equilibrium. From this view of entrepreneurship, it is clearly vital that entrepreneurs should be able to operate unconstrained and unimpeded if the allocation of factors of production is to best meet the ever changing conditions of demand and supply in order to maximize welfare for the population as a whole.

The *catalytic* entrepreneurs derived from Schumpeter's analysis create new production possibilities, ideas and concepts, but the *allocating* entrepreneurs from the Austrian school of thought observe the changes in conditions and are alert to the opportunities that they present. They are allocating entrepreneurs because they realize new ideas and concepts through innovation in economic activity. Catalysts are necessary but not sufficient for economic development —allocators are required to put the new concepts into practice.

The activities of catalytic and allocating entrepreneurs put pressure on traditional and existing businesses in the affected markets. The arrival of new firms in a market or new technologies in an industry increases the level of competition, thus putting pressure on existing businesses. To understand the implications of higher levels of competition and the reactions of existing firms, it is useful to consider the concept of X-inefficiency introduced by Harvey Leibenstein.

Coping with competitive pressure in existing businesses

Leibenstein noticed that contrary to the predictions of traditional economics, manufacturing plants that were identical in terms of their plant, equipment and levels of employment produced significantly different levels of output. Production plants differed in terms of their efficiency, and these variations were not explicable through differences in the allocation of plant and equipment and the number of people employed. There was clearly an element of efficiency that was not related to the way productive resources were allocated. Leibenstein termed this efficiency *X-efficiency*. Leibenstein explained variations in levels of X-efficiency in terms of competitive pressure, motivation and the seeking out and use of market information. More significant for individual competitiveness is the concept of *X-inefficiency*. Viewed in terms of X-inefficiency, lower levels of competitive pressure both outside and inside the firm would lead to lower levels of motivation while higher levels of ignorance as to changing conditions in the market place would reduce management efficiency. Basically there would tend to be more slack in the system in those businesses which confronted lower levels of competitive pressure and which were less aware of external events.

Leibenstein's perceptions are useful for our analysis here since they provide a further motive for entrepreneurial activity. As catalytic events are innovated through allocating entrepreneurs, they put pressure on existing established businesses that are then forced to refine their operations. The resources in these businesses may be allocated in the appropriate proportions but entrepreneurial activity can seek to reduce the levels of X-inefficiency that exist in the organization. In short, the changing competitive pressures brought about by catalytic and allocating entrepreneurship cause entrepreneurial activity in existing businesses as they are forced to refine their operations and reduce the amount of slack in their operating systems—this activity is defined as *refining* entrepreneurship.

Recent conjectures from business research by Amar Bhidé

Starting in 1988, Amar Bhidé began an in-depth study spanning a decade of hundreds of startup businesses and found that the understanding of entrepreneurship emerging from his data did not fit into the neat economic models of the 1980s. These have difficulty dealing with the classical entrepreneurial functions of coordination, arbitrage, innovation, and operating under conditions of uncertainty, according to economics professor William J. Baumol at the New York University. In 1993, in *Entrepreneurship, Management, and the Structure of Payoffs*, Baumol described this climate as, "Large companies have transformed innovation into a routine and predictable process that lends itself to the humdrum talents of capable managers."

Bhidé distinguishes between three different types of business phases involved in entrepreneurship, with very different characteristics (Ref. 2.6):

1. Most startups come from enthusiastic individuals seeking self-employment. They start their businesses by copying or slightly modifying someone else's ideas, and they do not usually have extensive managerial or industry experience, both of which are barriers to obtaining outside funding. Their modest enterprises are financed from personal assets such as savings and mortgages on their homes. The median startup capital is around $10,000. The successful new entrepreneurs operate in market niches with a high degree of uncertainty due to changing technology and changing customer wants but with a chance of securing a large payoff. However, they do not have the resources for research or planning. A key characteristic is their high tolerance for ambiguity and for "learning by doing." According to Bidhé, "Entrepreneurs who effectively adapt to unexpected problems and opportunities and who persuade resource providers to take a chance on their startups can influence their luck. Personal traits such as open-mindedness, the willingness to make decisions quickly, the ability to cope with setbacks and rejections, and skill in face-to-face selling help differentiate the winners from the also-rans."

2. Entrepreneurs who are building a long-lived firm from a startup require different traits than those needed at startup. They are not necessarily the initial founders but the individuals holding a significant economic stake in the business and in control of its operation. They must have strong ambitions and audacious goals, with a willingness to take personal risks. They must be able to imaginatively make the future conform to their vision and creatively integrate ideas from many sources. They must learn new business and administrative skills few founders possess initially. In addition, they must develop a business strategy and a firm commitment to implement it through inspiring leadership and persuasion. Only a small number of startup entrepreneurs go on to build their business into a significant enterprise. Typically, it takes decades for these companies to develop their assets and organization into a leader in their field.

3. Entrepreneurial conditions in large corporations are quite different. Champions of new initiatives must conduct extensive research and set up detailed plans to reduce uncertainty and document the likelihood of profits to obtain approval for their projects. Success then hinges on the participation and cooperation of many individuals and teams. These projects will have much larger funding available but at a loss of flexibility for course changes once the project is launched. Contrary to Schumpeter's view, innovations in large corporations are usually routine and involve many small steps rather than a single catalytic event. New ideas will only gradually replace existing products and processes since the corporations do not want to jeopardize the profits from their current products.

Synthesis

Having considered the three distinct types of entrepreneurial activity—catalytic, allocating, and refining—we can now observe the full implications of a creative leap or inspiration in three terms: (a) the catalytic effect it has upon economic development potential, (b) the actual effect realized through allocating activity and (c) the efficiency effects resulting from the refinement of traditional business operations. It also helps us to understand how we as individuals might fit into this process, whether as a founder to start up a business, an entrepreneur building a business, or an intrapreneur championing innovation in a large corporation. Creativity and effective problem solving are required at all points. Although most clearly observable in the generation of catalytic events, ideas and concepts, creativity and effective problem solving are also needed by allocating entrepreneurs if the developmental potential of these events is to be realized and by refining entrepreneurs as they confront the new problems facing their business. Individuals may also fall into more that one category. The concept originator may go on to realize its profit-generating potential and thus creates the economic development that it makes possible. The important point here is that creativity and effective problem solving are indelibly linked with entrepreneurial activity in all its forms. The question of what constitutes, enables, and encourages creativity is explored next.

Creativity in the entrepreneurial process

Before we proceed any further, we need to stop and consider the definitions of creativity, invention, and innovation and how these concepts relate to entrepreneurship.

What is creativity?

The word *creativity* is derived from the Latin *creare* to make and the Greek *kreinein* to fulfill. Creativity can be examined from each of these perspectives. Creativity enables us to make something new and hitherto unimagined. In the context of entrepreneurship, it is creativity that leads to the development of new products and processes which when innovated replace the traditional and previous version. Creativity leads to greater fulfillment on an individual basis as we use our imagination to create new horizons in terms of what we do in our lives. Through our imagination of what we could be and achieve, we move beyond the boundaries that we have previously set ourselves. Creativity therefore has a novelty and also relevance in terms of changing what we do and what we believe about our potential, which is yet to be realized.

Where does creativity come from?

An essential quality of creativity is that it involves the unexpected, the new and the surprising. As a result this has been attributed to many different sources.

> *I must give up everything else to develop and cultivate the germ that God has planted in me.*
> Tchaikovsky

- **Divine Inspiration** – Creativity is seen as "higher-order" thinking or divination.

- **Serendipity** – Here creativity is seen as the product of a fortuitous coincidence of thoughts and events. For example, saccharin was discovered accidentally by a chemist who happened to eat his lunch in the laboratory. He had failed to wash his hands before eating after undertaking experiments involving the components of the sweetener.

- **Contrived Luck** – Here creativity is seen as the natural outcome of a more systematic approach to generate conditions conducive to creativity. This involves a mindset that deliberately explores existing conditions and scans for opportunities. In such a climate, creativity is more likely to occur and the frequency of those events will be greater. For example, companies such as 3M, Hewlett-Packard and Glaxo have designed organizational cultures to ensure that "luck" is a highly probable and frequent occurrence.

> *In the fields of observation, chance favors only the mind that is prepared.*
> Louis Pasteur

- **Determinism** – Under this view and interpretation, creativity is "forced" via tenacious determination to solve a particular problem. The desired outcome is seen to eventually determines the creative ideas that enable it to happen for the first time.

- **Learning Processes** – In this case it is accepted that high levels of creativity are associated with particular processes that characterize the way we think and behave. Sources of this way of thinking can be identified and lead to the possibility for learning to be more creative. In some ways this view reflects an acceptance of the effectiveness of contrived luck and determinism since it refers to a variety of techniques that can be applied to encourage creative problem solving. This perception underpins much of the approach adopted in this book and constitutes the link between creativity, entrepreneurship and innovation in practice.

How are creativity and innovation related?

Ned Herrmann (1922-1999), the inventor of whole-brain technology and the Herrmann Brain Dominance Instrument (HBDI), saw creativity as a dynamic, whole-brain activity that involves conscious and subconscious mental processing in both generating an idea and making something happen as a result. Creativity rarely occurs in isolation—it needs other people's minds, ideas, and inventions. Thus in the broadest perspective, creativity is expressed in the quality of the solutions we develop in problem solving. Creativity also involves looking beyond the obvious and is a necessary condition for invention or innovation. Because the word *creativity* carries with it a value judgment, Edward de Bono uses the neutral label of *lateral thinking* to describe the change from one way of looking at things to another.

Innovation can be seen as the practical application of creativity in an organization. Creativity originates in an individual mind (often enhanced by group interaction and synthesis), but innovation usually requires the involvement of a team and subsequently a wider organization. As we shall see later in this chapter, good communication is central to innovation. Businesses often use the terms *creativity* and *innovation* interchangeably, because many managers feel more comfortable with the word *innovation*. One key difference between the two processes is timing—creativity is needed in the early stages of product development, whereas innovation occurs much later and usually in a broader context. Innovation builds on a creative idea, or it can combine creative ideas in novel ways. In general, innovation is much safer; it is incremental; it is building on an already established product or process, and it is far easier to achieve successfully than creating something new where a successful outcome is by no means assured and the possibility of failure must be acknowledged. The two processes are championed by different types of entrepreneurs—the adaptive (or allocating) entrepreneur to shepherd innovation, the inventive (or catalytic) entrepreneur to chart or envision new paths.

Who are the inventors and innovators, and what are their common traits?

Conventional wisdom says that if you want to invent something highly technical, you must have extensive technical knowledge in the subject area. Yet many inventors are outsiders; they learn on their own and create knowledge as they go along. Developing inventions into more useful and more sophisticated products is another story; this usually happens through many successive improvements and innovative steps by people with expertise in the relevant areas of science and engineering. For example, the Wright Brothers invented the first successful airplane, but it took thousands of Boeing engineers to design and build the 747 jumbo jets to fly non-stop across the Pacific. Chester Carlson invented the Xerox process, but it took years of development at Battelle to produce a practical copier. Whereas Alistair Pilkington thought of the idea of float glass while helping his wife wash dishes, it took a team of six people working in secret for seven years (and a huge

> *A company cannot expect creative acts in a particular area to come only from the experts in that area.*
> *The problem with expertise lies precisely in those grooved-in patterns and scripts that make people experts in the first place.*
>
> A. Robinson and S. Stern (Ref. 2.1)

research budget) to develop the process into a technical and commercial success. A key ingredient was the optimism maintained by the team while struggling to overcome problem after problem. Art Fry was the inventor of the Post-it note, but it took teams of people at 3M to turn the invention into a line of successful business products. Characteristic common traits of inventors, innovators and many entrepreneurs are listed in Table 2.1.

Table 2.1 *Common Traits of Inventors, Innovators and Entrepreneurs*

- Curious—looking at the frontiers of knowledge; eager to learn.
- Inventing to satisfy a need or solving problems creatively.
- Looking for new ways and many approaches for doing things.
- Observing trends, looking for opportunities, then working hard.
- Realizing that most progress is made in small steps through continuous improvement.
- Dedicated and passionate about their projects, with low need for status and power and low vulnerability to rejection.
- Having a sense of value, integrity, purpose and humor; being hands-on and flexible.
- Being self-confident, independent, courageous, persistent, reliable, and tenacious.
- Not afraid to take risks and make mistakes; questioning conventional wisdom.
- Tolerance for ambiguity; able to deal with contradictory information; imaginative.

Especially in academia, researchers are often more interested in discovery and invention for the sake of new knowledge than in subsequent technology transfer, because commercialization of a creative idea requires a different mindset, as we shall see in Chapter 3. Governments in many industrialized countries are providing funds in an effort to increase the flow of commercially viable ideas from their academic institutions to spur economic development. Businesses with ability for innovation have a distinct advantage in an increasingly global competition—a lack of innovation can lead to stagnation and imperil the survival of the business.

> *The basic aim of education is not to accumulate knowledge, but rather to learn to think creatively, teach oneself, and "seek answers to questions as yet unexplored."*
>
> Jim Killian, former president of MIT

Overcoming barriers to creative thinking—for individuals

It is now generally accepted that most people are born with the capacity to think creatively, but that through influences at home, in school, and in their particular culture they bury their natural creativity. We believe that these barriers to creativity can be overcome and that we can learn to be lateral thinkers. We will briefly examine three types of barriers: false assumptions, habits, and emotions.

False assumptions barrier

Here are some examples of false assumptions.

• The belief that *we are not creative* is a self-fulfilling prophecy. This assumption is false, because we have an astounding potential to be creative and can learn to unlock or hone our creative thinking skills.

• Edward de Bono has shown that *an intelligent mind is a good thinker* is a false assumption for a number of reasons, such as mistaking verbal fluency for good thinking, arguing a case for a certain point of view well and thus failing to see the need to explore alternatives, or jumping to quick conclusions from a few data points.

• The attitude that *play is frivolous* is a false assumption prevalent in the business world, in schools, and often among parents as well. Yet unstructured play is very important to our cognitive development. Humor is related to play and beneficial to creative thinking because it turns the mind from the usual, expected track to making an unexpected lateral leap.

We can overcome false assumptions by spending time with creative people—we can let them be our mentors and find out what it means to express and champion creative ideas. We can play with ideas, analogies, and metaphors. We can frequently exercise our imagination by asking what-if questions. We can practice new creative thinking and problem-solving modes!

Learned habits barriers

Activity 2.2: Symbols Problem

Circle the figure below that is different from all the others, then explain why.

a. △   b. ☐   c. ○   d. ∩   e. +

Reason: _____

The correct answer to the symbols problem is that *all are different*. Can you find reasons to explain why each of the symbols is different from all the others? Most people stop after finding one answer, because we have not been trained to look for alternatives. This little exercise illustrates that different answers can be correct or appropriate depending on the questions being asked or the criteria being used.

Here are examples of mental barriers that are often learned in school:

• *There is only one right answer* is a serious barrier when we are dealing with other than purely mathematical problems. Looking for alternatives is especially important when dealing with ideas. How do we know our answer is best if we have nothing to compare it with?

• *Looking at a problem in isolation* is a related mental block. When you look at the previous pages, how many rectangles do you see? Most people would say *four* (the textboxes and the symbol shown in item b of the activity). Or was your answer *six* (if you saw the two open pages) or *seven* if you considered the two pages together as an additional rectangle? What if you included other rectangles in your field of vision in the room (and outside): windows, checkered shirts, papers, boxes, shelves, floor or ceiling tiles, and so on? Before we can find answers to a problem, we must find out if the problem is part of a larger problem. The context is never irrelevant! Having a very narrow point of view can be a mental barrier to creative thinking and easily happens when we have become experts in our work.

• *Following the rules* is a mental block that requires wisdom to overcome. Sometimes, before we can come up with truly novel ideas, we must question existing constraints. Also, we have to make sure we do not make up our own rules and barriers. Are the "rules" we put on others or ourselves really necessary or helpful? When we do not question arbitrary criteria, we may miss opportunities for creative thinking and improvements. Sometimes we follow rules when the original reason no longer exists. The classic example is the QWERTY system for arranging the letters on a computer keyboard. It was originally invented to slow down typists because the typewriter keys were jamming when they typed too fast. However, some constraints are necessary. For example, when working with others, following the rules of etiquette for courteous behavior creates a safer, less stressful environment for creativity. As we shall see in Chapter 4, rules and problem solving paradigms are generally useful and practical to function well in our daily routines.

We can overcome habit barriers that have been taught by explicitly looking for a broad context and seeking different alternatives, analyzing the purpose of rules and deciding which should be suspended in the initial stages of problem solving.

Attitude barriers

This group of mental blocks is difficult to deal with because it involves our attitudes and emotions. Let us briefly examine some examples.

* *Negative, pessimistic thinking* (including criticism, sarcasm and put-downs) are mental blocks that not only inhibit creative thinking in the person using them—they have the same effect on all those coming in contact with the negative thinker and are thus doubly destructive. It is so easy to focus on small shortcomings of an idea (or person) rather than recognize the good features. This influence starts at a young age: a typical child may receive a vast

> *To overcome a spirit of criticism and negative thinking, look at things as being different or interesting—not good or bad!*
>
> Edward de Bono

number of negative reactions for every positive reinforcement. Remember that a judgmental attitude, including our own inner "critical voice" can be powerful barriers against expressing creative thoughts.

* *Risk-avoidance or the fear of failure or rejection* prevents creative thinking as well as action. Examples of the kinds of risks we are talking about here are: speaking out in a group when you have an idea, even though it might be "hooted" down; learning something new where you will often fail until you become good at it, or standing up against peer pressure. Yes, you have to stick your neck out when you champion a creative idea; you also need a thick shell, and you have to be persistent in getting to your goal. If you do not encounter critics trying to make "turtle soup" out of you, your idea probably was not that creative! The need for "being cool" and being accepted by one's peer group is especially strong among young people who are particularly vulnerable to rejection.

We can overcome attitude barriers by encouraging people around us with positive feedback when they share creative ideas. We can take risks with learning and use failure creatively as a stepping-stone to success. We can practice out-of-the-box thinking daily! We can recognize flaws as opportunities for improvement! In the same way that athletes practice mental toughness to succeed among fierce competitors, we can adopt traits of mental toughness when developing a creative thinking mindset.

Innovation in an organization

This section does not give a recipe for building a creative and innovative business or organization or team—it will provide guidelines that will improve the chances for innovation to take place.

> We are becoming increasingly convinced that tomorrow's winners in business will be those who master the challenges of innovation and creativity and can do so continuously. Innovation is an engine for growth and value in business.
>
> Prof. Robert Goffee,
> London Business School,
> RSA Lecture, Jan 2000

Although creative acts seem random, their frequency can be increased by optimizing the four conditions or "pillars" that can sustain creativity and innovation. In all organizations, the creative potential represented by its people far exceeds the performance. This potential can be tapped and developed. The term intrapreneur has been coined to describe entrepreneurial thinkers and entrepreneurial champions in large organizations.

Pillar 1: Education

Since invention and innovation come from people who can think creatively, it seems that educating and training people in creative thinking and creative problem solving would be an obvious first step. However, even large companies rarely offer or encourage their employees to take such courses or workshops, yet this education must become part of an organization's culture if it wants to increase its chances for creativity beyond a hit-or-miss effort. Managers and work teams must have a common understanding and shared values about creativity and innovation. Learning, applying, encouraging and valuing creative thinking and creative problem solving skills becomes the responsibility of each individual—this then creates a positive climate for people who are "different" and can become models for generating and expressing creative ideas. There is an additional factor involved here—innovation involves change. As a consequence the learning requirements for major innovation are high for everyone affected by the innovation.

Pillar 2: Application in problem solving

Innovation is fostered when teams are trained and are routinely using the creative problem solving process. Teams are cross-functional, and innovation is a shared process. Teams understand that its members have different thinking preferences. An organization can offer training in creative thinking and a supportive climate, but if the problem-solving tools that are used routinely are strictly analytical, the likelihood of innovation will be significantly reduced. It is possible for creativity and innovation to "spiral up" into an entire organization from a successful smaller group that has started the creative process and developed an important out-of-the-box solution (for example, for a company's new product line).

Pillar 3: Organizational climate

Innovation occurs when organizations function as effective learning systems, and learning comes through experimentation and failure. According to Michael Tushman and David Nadler (Ref. 2.2), truly innovative organizations are those where people can take risks, reap the rewards of success, and survive constructive failures. Innovation entails risk. In order for innovation to flourish, society and

> *You can provide an environment in which creativity will flourish.*
> Allen F. Jacobson, CEO, 3M Company

organizations must have a certain tolerance for failure for those that try something new. Charles Prather and Lisa Gundry (Ref. 2.3) have identified nine dimensions that are characteristic of innovative organizations, as listed in Table 2.2.

Table 2.2 *Nine Dimensions of an Innovative Organizational Climate*

1. Challenge and involvement—"stretch" goals
2. Freedom—independence and autonomy
3. Time for new ideas
4. Support for new ideas
5. Positive conflict resolution
6. Debate—appreciation for diverse views
7. Playfulness and humor
8. Trust and openness
9. Protection for taking calculated risks

The best reward for innovators is to see their ideas implemented. The right people need to be rewarded—the originator as well as the developers (they are not usually the same persons). The emphasis must be on the quality of ideas, not quantity. The organizational climate should contain social pressure against NOT being creative. Managers who model these values and support innovation in their daily actions are the most effective. For example, employees became convinced that their manager was serious about his talk on taking risks when he handed each person two "Forgiveness Coupons" and told them these were his permission to make a mistake without any threat of retribution or blame. Then he added the clincher, "and you are expected to use both coupons by the end of the year."

Pillar 4: Communication

Communication is a critical link between education, application and climate and between individuals, teams, and management. Creative and innovative ideas must be communicated well to eventually become incorporated into business plans. Also, one person's failed experiment can become another's idea generator—if the information is communicated. According to Ikujro Nonaka and Hirotaka Takeuchi (Ref. 2.4),

> *The essence of innovation is to re-create the world according to a particular ideal or vision. Creating new knowledge is also not simply a matter of learning from others or acquiring knowledge from the outside. Knowledge has to be built on its own, frequently requiring intensive and laborious interaction among members of the organization. When organizations innovate, they do not simply process information—from the outside in—to solve existing problems or adapt to a changing environment. They actually create new knowledge and information—from the inside out—to redefine both problems and solutions and, in the process, to recreate their environment.*

At 3M, researchers are rewarded not just for discoveries but also for communicating them. New technologies are shared within the company. Anyone can talk to anybody else who is an expert in the company. People are valuable resources and are given time to respond to a call for assistance or request for information. "Creativity clubs" and "technology user groups" are excellent communication forums to foster exchange of ideas, continuous improvement, and innovation. Because it is easier to communicate with people who have similar thinking styles, managers must resist the temptation to hire people who are like them—to innovate successfully, it is crucial to purposefully hire and promote people who are "different" (Ref. 2.5)!

As an organization, you don't always have to innovate from within. You can be creative in recognizing opportunities and importing innovation. Bill Gates of Microsoft imported the disk-operating system (DOS). Examples of innovations that were recognized and adopted successfully by others are *Windows* (discarded by Xerox) and the quartz watch (unappreciated and left unprotected by the Swiss watch industry). Although Motorola invented six major innovations in its first 13 years of existence, it invented only five innovations in the next 42 years. However, the company has been prolific in acquiring new technologies from small firms and universities, over 250 just in the last two years, including machine vision, methanol fuel cells, SiGe-C semiconductor technology and a gel-based biochip.

Excessive control, a short-term view, being risk-averse, and a rigid political climate are barriers to innovation—in teams, organization, entire societies and cultures. Perhaps the most pervasive hindrance of all is the lack of information sharing, because it affects all three pillars.

Readling list for further learning

2.1   A. Robinson and S. Stern, Corporate Creativity: *How Innovation and Improvements Actually Happen*, Berrett-Koehler Publishers, Inc., San Francisco, 1997. This is a practical book for managers, with many detailed examples to help unleash the creative potential in companies.

2.2   Michael Tushman and David Nadler, *How Organizations Learn* (Ken Starkey, editor), International Thomson Business Press, 1996. An updated version subtitled *Managing the Search for Knowledge* is scheduled to come out soon.

2.3   Charles W. Prather and Lisa K. Gundry, *Blueprints for Innovation: How Creative Processes Can Make You and Your Company More Competitive*, American Management Association, New York, 1995. Concise and useful!

2.4   Ikujiro Nonaka and Hirotaka Takeuchi, *The Knowledge-Creating Company: How Japanese Companies Create the Dynamics of Innovation*, Oxford University Press, New York, 1995. The authors show, through a theoretical model and many case studies (which include organizations in the US) how Japanese companies create new knowledge and use it to manufacture successful products and develop innovative technologies.

2.5   Jerry Hirshberg, *The Creative Priority: Driving Innovative Business in the Real World*, HarperBusiness, New York, 1998. The founder and president of Nissan Design International reveals his strategy for designing an organization around creativity.

2.6   Amar V. Bhidé, *The Origin and Evolution of New Businesses*, Oxford University Press, 2000. The editor-in-chief of *Inc. Magazine,* George Gendron, calls this book "the single most signigficant combination to our understanding of entrepreneauship to date."

2.7   Genrich Altshuller (translated by Lev Shulyak), *And Suddenly the Inventor Appeared: TRIZ, the Theory of Inventive Problem Solving*, Technical Innovation Center, Inc., Worcester, Massachusetts, 1994. This is *the* manual on the TRIZ method.

2.8   W. S. Sahlman et al., *The Entrepreneurial Venture*, Harvard Business School Press, 2nd ed., 1999. This collection of readings is a comprehensive resource for entrepreneurs from generating ideas to preparing a business plan, raising funds and managing a growing enterprise.

Creative and visual thinking exercises

Warm-Ups: Don't just go with the first or obvious answer—play with many possibilities. Make sketches to help you visualize the problem; you will be surprised how fast the answers will come.

a. Recorded on side A of an old 45-rpm record is a musical number that lasts three minutes and twenty seconds. How many grooves are there on side A of this old record? _____

b. In a large box, there are six boxes, each of which contains three small boxes. How many boxes are there in all? _____

c. How do you keep fish from smelling? _____
_____

d. A man went into a hardware store and priced certain items. He was told they were 25 cents each. He replied, "I would like one hundred, please." The clerk rung up 75 cents on the register for the entire purchase. What did the man buy? _____

e. Two cities are exactly 100 miles apart. Charley leaves City A driving at 30mph and Bertha leaves City B 30 minutes later driving 60 mph. Who will be closer to City A when they meet? _____

f. A boy and a girl born on the same day of the same year with the same parents are not twins. How is this possible? _____

g. Three friends are on a bike trip. When a severe storm threatens, they decide to rent a room in a lodge instead of camping out. The proprietor quotes a price of £30 for the room, so each bicyclist digs out a ten-pound note. Later, the proprietor finds that he has overcharged the group by £5 and sends the errand boy to their room with the change. The boy—of a practical mindset—thinks that the three guests would have a hard time dividing up £5; thus he helps himself to two pounds (as a tip) and returns three pounds to the guests. This means that each person in essence would have paid £9, with the errand boy having pocketed an additional £2, for a total of £29. Where did the remaining pound disappear? _____
_____
_____
_____

Geese and Lambs: A farmer's child received a gift of 8 animals (geese and lambs) with a total of 22 legs. Determine the number of geese in at least three very different ways. _____

_____

_____

_____

_____

_____

_____

_____

_____

_____

_____

_____

_____

The Fastball Problem: The players form teams of 10 to 15 each. Each team is given a ball and players are asked to stand in a circle and count off. The object of this game is to have everybody on the team touch the ball in order. Time starts with the first touch and ends with the last. Each team passes the ball around the circle as fast as possible, like a hyperactive bucket brigade fighting a fire. The typical winning team takes just under 45 seconds. However, one winning team takes just two seconds. Impossible! No, there are at least two ways this can be achieved. Can you come up with a solution? Use a rolled up wad of paper and experiment, then sketch or describe your idea. _____

_____

_____

_____

_____

_____

_____

_____

_____

_____

_____

_____

_____

Mountain Path Problem: Read through the following story. Jot down notes in the box below on the different ways you are thinking about the problem, even if you are not able to come up with a solution.

A certain mountain in Nepal has a shrine at its peak and only one narrow path to reach it. A monk leaves his monastery at the base of the mountain at 6 o'clock one morning and ascends the mountain at a steady pace. After some hours, he tires and takes a long rest. Then he resumes his climb, albeit more slowly, and he pauses often to meditate. Finally, at sunset, he reaches the shrine where he spends the night. At sunrise, he begins his descent, quickly at first, and then more slowly as his knees begin to ache. After a couple of rest stops, he accelerates his pace again— he does not want to miss dinner at the monastery. Prove that there is a point in the path that the monk reached at exactly the same time of day on his way up and on his way down.

Lateral thinking exercises

a. The butcher at Tony's Meat Market is 41 years old, 6 ft 2 inches tall, wears an extra-large shirt and a size 46 shoe. What does he weigh? _____

b. Here is an equation of Roman numerals, made with 10 sticks. It is incorrect. Can you correct the equation without touching the sticks, adding new sticks, or taking away any sticks?

$$XI + I = X$$

c. Shown below is a Roman numeral nine. By adding only a single line, turn it into a six. Can you find at least two different ways for solving this problem?

I X

_____

_____

d. How many times can you take three from 25? _____

e. Take two apples from five apples. How many do you have? _____

f. A plane with English tourists on board flies from Holland to Spain. It crashes in France. Where should the survivors be buried? _____

_____

g. What do you sit on, sleep on, and brush your teeth with?_____

_____

h. How many letters are in Mississippi? _____

Sentence Problem:

In how many ways can you complete the following sentence to get a true statement? Enter your answers below.

This statement has _____ "t" letters.

_____

_____

_____

_____

_____

_____

_____

_____

_____

_____

_____

_____

_____

Geometric Problems:

A. Divide the triangle into four
   identical pieces.

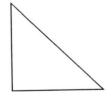

B. Divide the trapezoidal shape into
   five identical pieces.

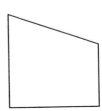

C. Divide the C shape into six
   identical pieces.

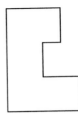

D. Divide the hexagon into eight
   identical symmetric pieces.

E. Divide the hexagon into eight
   asymmetric but identical pieces.

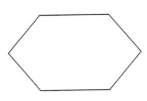

F. Divide the "lozenge" into nine
   identical pieces.

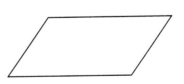

Inventive Thinking Exercises

1. The Missing Baseball Problem: Inventive thinking is not limited to adults but can be done by people of all ages, as illustrated by this problem. A young boy loved to play baseball, and he took his bat and balls everywhere. However, when visiting his grandmother one day, he discovered that he had brought his bat but had forgotten his balls. To prevent this from happening again, he came up with an invention (which he patented and is now sold by Toys-R-Us). What did he invent? _____

_____

_____

_____

2. The Hanging Chain Problem: Imagine being in a totally empty room except for two chains that are hanging from the ceiling. If you grab one by the hand and move toward the other, it is still about a foot too far away for you to reach with your other hand. Yet the assignment is to tie the two chains together. Describe or sketch at least two different solutions to solve the problem. Hint: What is the *real* problem? _____

_____

_____

_____

_____

3. Moving the Transformer Problem: A transformer weighing two tons sits on a free-standing platform 4 ft above ground. Find two ways for lowering the transformer to the ground without using a crane and without destroying the platform or the transformer. Then discuss which of the solutions you consider to be superior and why. _____

_____

_____

_____

_____

_____

_____

_____

4. **The Chocolate Candy Problem:** You have brought a big box of chocolate candies to a party. These candies are shaped like small bottles and are filled with thick raspberry syrup. When you pass the box around, one of your friends wonders how the syrup was placed in the candy. Can you think of at least two ways that these candies could be made? Which of your solutions would be the easiest and most economical to produce? Would your solution work if the filling were cherry brandy, or how would you have to change it? _____

_____

_____

_____

_____

_____

_____

_____

_____

5. **The Dripping Paint Problem:** Have you ever been annoyed at the paint dripping off a roller as you transferred it from the pan to the wall you were working on? Think of an inventive approach that would eliminate the problem (but would still use the roller concept). _____

_____

_____

_____

6. **The Sticky Window Problem.** A certain brand of casement windows is shipped from the factory with four 10-cm wide blocks of styrofoam attached at the top and bottom of the frame to allow stacking the windows without damaging the crank and handle hardware? A very sticky adhesive is left on the frame when the blocks are removed to install the windows. How would you solve this problem?

_____

_____

_____

_____

_____

_____

Answers to the creative and visual thinking exercises

Warm-Ups:

a. Draw the track of the needle. Can you see the answer? One groove!

b. There are 25 boxes in all—one plus six plus eighteen. Again, did you draw a picture? If not, draw one now and see how easy the question becomes.

c. Cook it when you catch it; freeze it; wrap it in paper; leave it in the water; switch to eating chicken; keep a cat around; burn incense; cut of its nose. Does this give you some additional ideas?

d. He bought three house numbers to make up the numeral 100.

e. You do not need to do any math—in fact, that mental language is a hindrance in this case. No matter how fast the two people travel or in which direction, at the moment they meet, they will be (by definition) in the same place and thus the same distance from City A.

f. They are two of a set of triplets, or two of a set of quadruplets, or …

g. Here it helps to have a consistent viewpoint: Guests: They paid £27; then *subtract* the boy's tip to get a room price of £25. Proprietor: He took in £30 and returned £5 (for a room price of £25) of which three pounds went to the guests and two to the boy.

Geese and Lambs:

1. Use algebra: make up two equations with two unknowns:
   x = number of lambs, y = number of geese.
   $x + y = 8$ (animals) and $4x + 2y = 22$ (legs).
   Multiply the first equation by 2 and subtract from the second:
   $4x - 2x + 2y - 2y = 22 - 2 \times 8 = 6.$
   Therefore, $x = 3$ and $y = 5$. Check: $4 \times 3 + 2 \times 5 = 22.$

2. Use trial and error.

3. Use tabulation: Keep the total number of animals constant, start with maximum number of lamb legs (32) and corresponding geese legs (0); then 28 lamb legs and 2 geese legs, then 24 lamb legs and 4 geese legs, and so on, to 12 lamb legs and 10 geese legs (which gives the desired total of 22 legs). The tabulation could have been done in the other direction, or by keeping the number of legs constant and varying the number of animals.

4. Use a graph, with the total number of legs on one axis and the number of geese on the other axis. Then plot the number of legs of 0 geese (and 8 lambs) = 32, 1 goose (and 7 lambs) = 32, etc. until 5 geese (and 3 lambs) = the desired 22 legs.

5. The easiest visualization is this (invented by an elementary school child): Draw 8 circles representing the animals. Draw two legs on each circle, since the animals have at least two legs each. This makes a total of 16 legs. Then add two legs to one circle at a time, until 22 legs have been drawn. You will then have three circles with four legs (or three lambs), with five circles remaining that have only two legs (or five geese).

6. Other answers are possible, including using real animals or toys.

Conclusion: Many ways of thinking are useful and valid for solving problems. The way we solve problems depends on our thinking preferences and on the methods we have been taught.

Mountain Path Problem:

Many people have trouble coming up with a solution. This is expected since the answer cannot be reasoned out with verbal, sequential thinking. Some people may use trial-and-error and make up a specific example with distances and times, but such a complicated approach is not necessary—we are seeking a general solution. The most common visual solution is usually some type of graph of height versus time, where varying slopes of the lines indicate the different speeds of going up and coming down. The slopes do not influence the essence of the answer—the spot where the two lines intersect. This visualization is still difficult for some, especially non-technical folks. But when given another way to look at the problem, everyone immediately "sees" the answer. Imagine merging the two days, with two people on the path, one going up and one coming down. They will have to meet at some point on the path, at some time during the day. Through visualization and imagination, we can reframe problems to where it is much easier to see solutions.

The Fastball Problem:

One solution is to place the ball in the center of a circle where the team members place their hands on it in sequence (and very quickly) while standing very close to each other. Another solution is for the team to form a path for the ball to roll across (or drop down) either by using outstretched arms or outstretched index fingers—this depends somewhat on the size of the ball being used.

Answers to the lateral thinking exercises

a. The details of age, height, and size are setting us up to think in the context of personal descriptions, and the question is interpreted to refer to body weight. But if we are trying to think creatively, we want to resist the given context— or at least go beyond it to consider other interpretations. Thinking of the question in terms of "what does he spend his time weighing?" leads you to another answer—meat. Or simply visualize Tony at this job, selling meat to a customer. What is he putting on the scales?

b. To solve this problem, you have to break away from the obvious way of looking at things. If you look at a situation from only one perspective, it is like drawing a boundary around the way you think and working only within that boundary. You can solve this problem by looking at it in a new way. To make the equation correct, turn your book upside down, or hold the page up to a light and look at it from the backside. Did your mental blocks prevent you from trying these unfamiliar approaches?

c. You can draw a horizontal line through the IX. Then, when you turn the page around, you have the Roman numeral VI on top of the line. But let's think in a new context—away from Roman numerals. Add an "S" in front of the IX, and you have SIX.

d. We can take 3 from 25 only once, because then it becomes 22.

e. In math, the scheme we are taught is to look at what remains. But, if you take two apples from five apples, what you have in your hand is two apples.

f. Like the butcher who weighs meat, the way this problem is framed sets up one context (England, Holland, Spain, France—where?), but the solutions lies in being able to look beyond this to notice that survivors are not buried!

g. Beware the context and the thinking pattern this exercise has set up—it can lead to false assumptions. You have probably assumed that there had to be a single, common answer. The answer to the question is quite simply: a chair, a bed, and a toothbrush.

h. There are millions and millions of mail letters on desks and in file cabinets all over the State of Mississippi. The more easily you can slip from verbal thinking (letters and words) to visual thinking (envelopes with sheets of paper and a huge land area located in the Southern US, the more apt you are to "solve" problems like this one.

Geometric Problems:

The first five shapes take some thinking (and visualization) to solve, with various strategies like doodling and dividing into "lowest common denominators" and learning from the previous shapes. This, however, then creates a pitfall—to where we attempt to solve the last problem in a most complicated, instead of the easy way, by following previous patterns.

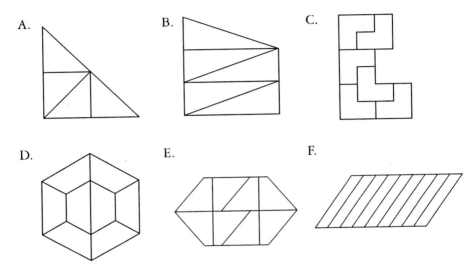

Sentence Problem:

This problem has many different answers. You can start with six lower-case or seven (including the upper-case) or eight "t" letters, but then you need to think out of the box. The sentence has *English typewritten "t" letters, black letters, serif style letters, no crooked or broken letters, handwritten and typed letters,* and so on.

Answers to the inventive thinking exercises

1. **The Missing Baseball Problem.** The boy invented a bat made out of a wide transparent handle section with a screw-on lid. Three brightly colored balls can be stored in the handle for transport (and visibility).

2. **The Hanging Chain Problem.** Try reframing the problem—or, what is the real problem? Depending on what you perceive to be the problem, your mind will find solutions in that direction. Here are three different solutions:

a. Are the chains too short? Tie your shoestrings or a piece of clothing to one of the chains; then pull that lengthened chain toward the other, which you are now able to grab.

b. Is the distance too far? Set the chains in motion toward each other to shorten the distance. If they are not heavy enough to move, tie your shoe(s) to one or both of them to make a better pendulum. When the chains are close together, grab them quickly before they swing in the opposite direction.

c. Are your arms too short? If you're a person with a flexible body and long legs (and good balance), you might be able to hook one chain with your foot.

3. **Moving the Transformer Problem.** The original problem and solution are embedded in the narrative of a true story, as told in the opening chapter of Reference 2.6. The inventive solution (by an accountant) consisted of blocks of ice stacked up carefully and built into a platform even with the transformer's platform. The ice tower was covered with a strong flat board, and the transformer was slid from its original position onto the board by workers using pry bars. The sun and warm night temperatures did the rest —by the end of the second day, all the ice had melted and the transformer arrived at ground level.

4. **The Chocolate Candy Problem.** Freeze the syrup and dip the syrup icicle into melted chocolate. The brandy could alternately be injected into the upright molded bottles, and then capped or closed off with a chocolate plug.

5. **The Dripping Paint Problem.** An innovative roller is being advertised for sale on US television (Spring 2002). The ad shows the paint being poured into a porous roller and then applied to the surface being painted when pressure is applied. Now why didn't we think of that?

6. **The Sticky Window Problem.** (a) Think of alternate, safe, inexpensive ways of packaging the windows for safe shipment. (b) Think of alternate ways of attaching the blocking (not requiring sticky adhesive). (c) Since a strong solvent might damage the finish on the window frame, think of ways to make the current adhesive "removable"? This is an example of a problem encountered recently by one of the authors during construction of a new church building. Develop a habit of being on the lookout for problems. Jot them down in your notebook. Either an inventive solution to an existing problem or an existing solution applied to an entirely different situation can become the seed for a new enterprise.

Entrepreneurship is an unrehearsed combination
of economic resources instigated by the uncertain prospect
of temporary monopoly profit.
Martin Binks and Philip Vale, 1990

Action checklist

➤   This section is full of action items and prompts. Skim back over the section and highlight those "things to do" that would benefit you most. Then select one that has a high potential for developing your thinking and behavior, and do it over the next three weeks.

➤   Place your watch on the opposite arm from where you usually wear it. Each time you look at it, let it serve as a reminder to check if you can incorporate creative thinking into your current activity.

➤   Schedule a one-hour "playing with ideas" time into your weekly calendar. Then keep your appointment! Keep a notebook with your most creative ideas. Be flexible, not perfect!

➤   Make a conscious effort to praise the creative thinking of another person, even if the occurrence annoys you. Example: A seven-year old youngster in your family uses the tea strainer for cleaning the cat's litter box (when she can't find the regular tool to do the assigned chore).

➤   Review your original definition of "entrepreneur." From what you have learned in this chapter, rewrite your definition, if possible in thirty words or less.

_____

_____

_____

_____

_____

_____

_____

_____

_____

_____

Chapter 3
The Herrmann Thinking Styles Model

As was shown in Chapter 2, entrepreneurship is indelibly linked to creativity and effective problem solving. In this chapter, we will see that the way people approach problem solving is strongly influenced by their preferred ways of thinking and "knowing." It has long been recognized that people vary significantly in their thinking styles, and models have been put forward in an attempt to capture these differences. The most familiar distinction (known since antiquity) is left-brain and right-brain thinking, where the left brain is considered to be analytical, systematic and logical, while the right brain is perceived as creative, artistic and intuitive. For our purposes, it is useful to go beyond this simple two-sided approach by adopting a *four-quadrant model of thinking* which enables a much clearer understanding of the creative problem solving process (described in Chapter 4) that will be used to generate and develop entrepreneurial ideas from "brain to market." As will be shown, this *creative problem solving model* can be applied to a wide variety of situations. The focus on entrepreneurship provides a powerful vehicle to convey the nature and effectiveness of the two models.

Our thinking styles characterize our approaches to problem solving. For example, one person may carefully analyze a situation before making a rational decision based on the available data; another may see the same situation in a broader context and will look for alternatives. One person will use a very detailed, cautious, step-by-step procedure; another has a need to talk the problem over with people and will solve the problem intuitively. All use their particular approaches based on successful experiences. We will now explore a model of thinking preferences that will help you learn to become a more effective thinker, problem solver, and entrepreneur.

> *Why are some people so smart and dull at the same time?*
> *How can they be so capable of certain mental activities and at the same time be so incapable of others?*
> Henry Mintzberg,
> *Harvard Business Review*
> July 1976

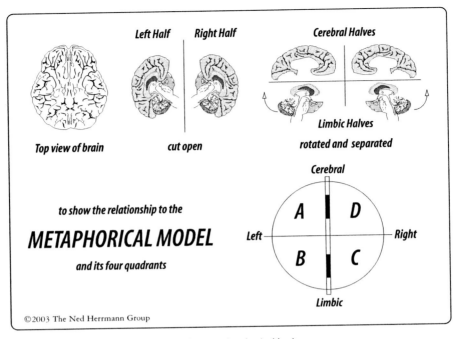

Figure 3.1 How the Herrmann model relates to the physical brain

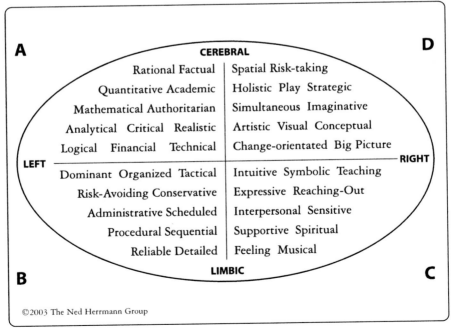

Figure 3.2 Thinking characteristics and behavioral clues of the Herrmann model

Development of the Herrmann model

Ned Herrmann earned a degree in physics and was hired by General Electric, where he soon worked in human resource development. In years of research into the creativity of the human brain, he came to recognize that the brain is specialized in the way it functions. These specialized modes can be modeled and organized into four distinct quadrants, each with its own language, values, and "ways of knowing."

Each person is a unique mix of these modes of thinking preferences and has one or more strong dominances. Dominance has advantages: quick response time and higher skill level, and we use our dominant mode for learning and problem solving. The stronger our preference for one way of thinking, the stronger is our discomfort for the opposite mode. "Opposite" people have great difficulty communicating and understanding each other because they see the world through very different "filters." Is there a best way? Ned Herrmann found that each brain mode is best for the tasks it was designed to perform. We must learn how to use and integrate these modes for whole-brain thinking and optimal problem solving.

When Ned Herrmann looked around for a method to diagnose thinking preferences based on brain specialization, he could not find any existing tools suitable for his purposes (since many tools such as the Myers-Briggs Type Indicator are based on psychological constructs). So he developed his own assessment, now known as the Herrmann Brain Dominance Instrument (HBDI™) which has been validated by scores of studies over many years. When the answers to 120 questions on the HBDI are scored by a computer at Herrmann International headquarters in North Carolina, the numerical results are also shown as a graphical profile. Recent advances in brain research support the validity of the descriptive model that divides the brain into left and right halves and into the cerebral and limbic hemispheres, resulting in four distinct quadrants, as shown in Figure 3.1 and Figure 3.2. For more detailed information on the HBDI, visit the web site at <u>www.hbdi.com</u>.

Although the four-quadrant model was organized based on the divisions in the physical brain, it is a *metaphorical* model—the newest imaging techniques show the brain's complexity, subtlety, and versatility involved in even the simplest thinking tasks. Yet, this simple model is useful for clarifying how we think, and it allows for the varied interrelationship of the different thinking abilities associated with each quadrant.

Strong as well as low preferences (akin to avoidances) are expressed in clues that can be observed in a person's behavior. The following sections describe the characteristics of each quadrant, together with typical average HBDI profiles of different occupational groups and activities to strengthen these thinking modes. In general, it is easier to develop competencies in areas of strong thinking preference.

Characteristics of quadrant A thinking

Quadrant A thinking is analytical, quantitative, technical, precise, logical, rational, and critical. Thus it deals with data analysis, risk assessment, statistics, financial budgets and computation, as well as with analytical problem solving, technical hardware, and making decisions based on logical reasoning. Quadrant A cultures are materialistic, academic, and authoritarian, and they are achievement-oriented and performance-driven. Examples of quadrant A thinkers are Star Trek's Mr. Spock, George Gallup the pollster, and Marilyn Vos Savant (a person with one of the highest IQ scores in the world). Engineers (see Figure 3.3), mathematicians, computer analysts, actuaries and accountants, and surgeons and pathologists generally show strong preferences for quadrant A thinking. People with quadrant A thinking talk about "the bottom line" or "getting the facts" or "critical analysis." Some learning activities preferred by quadrant A thinkers are listed in Table 3.1.

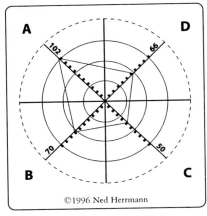

© 1996 Ned Herrmann

Figure 3.3 *Typical average HBDI profile for chemical engineers (Ref. 3.3)*

Table 3.1 *Quadrant A Learning Activities and Behaviors*

- Looking for data and information; doing library and web searches.
- Listening to informational lectures; reading textbooks.
- Analyzing (and studying) example problems and solutions.
- Doing research using the scientific method.
- Judging ideas based on facts, criteria, and logical reasoning.
- Doing technical and financial case studies.
- Knowing how things work and how much they cost.
- Dealing with hardware; answering "what" questions.
- Joining an investment club; financially planning your retirement.

Characteristics of quadrant B thinking

Quadrant B thinking is organized, sequential, controlled, planned, conservative, structured, detailed, and scheduled. It deals with administration, tactical planning, procedures, organizational form, maintaining the status quo, the "tried-and-true" and solution implementation. The culture is reliable, traditional, and bureaucratic. It is production-oriented and task-driven. Edgar

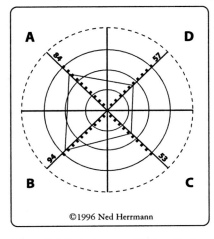

©1996 Ned Herrmann

Figure 3.4 *Typical average HBDI profile for manufacturing foremen (Ref. 3.3)*

Hoover, former FBI Director, Prince Otto von Bismarck, Prussian Chancellor of Germany (1871-1900), and the American Indian Chief Geronimo exemplify quadrant B thinkers. People who prefer quadrant B thinking want their jobs to be structured and sequentially organized. Planners, bureaucrats, administrators, bookkeepers, and clerks exhibit preferences for quadrant B thinking (see Figure 3.4). People with dominant quadrant B modes talk about "we have always done it this way" or "law and order" or "self-discipline" or "play it safe." Quadrant B learning activities are listed in Table 3.2.

Table 3.2 *Quadrant B Learning Activities and Behaviors*

- Doing detailed written work neatly and conscientiously.
- Doing lab work, step by step and then writing a sequential report.
- Using computers with tutorial software. Asking "how" questions.
- Organizing a collection (or a closet or drawer).
- Planning projects, then executing them according to plan.
- Practicing new skills through frequent repetition and drill.
- Assembling an object according to detailed instructions.
- Setting up a detailed budget and keeping track of expenditures.
- Setting up a filing system and then using it regularly.

Characteristics of quadrant C thinking

Quadrant C thinking is sensory, kinesthetic, emotional, people-oriented, and symbolic. It deals with awareness of feelings, body sensations, spiritual values, music, personal relationships, teamwork, nurturing, and communication.

Quadrant C cultures are humanistic, cooperative, and spiritual; they are feelings-oriented and value-driven. Dr. Martin Luther King, Jr., Princess Diana, and Mahatma Gandhi (Hindu social reformer) typify strong quadrant C people. People who prefer quadrant C thinking (see Figure 3.5) like the social sciences, music, dance, and highly skilled sports, and they prefer group projects to working alone. Elementary school and foreign language teachers, trainers, counselors, dental assistants, nurses, social workers, and musicians generally have strong preferences for interpersonal quadrant C thinking. People with quadrant C dominances talk about "the family" or "the team" or "personal growth" and "values." Table 3.3 lists some quadrant C learning activities.

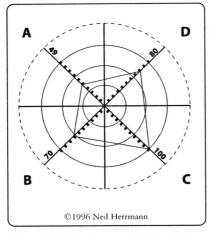

© 1996 Ned Herrmann

Figure 3.5 *Typical average HBDI profile for rehab counselors (Ref. 3.3)*

Table 3.3 *Quadrant C Learning Activities and Behaviors*

- Listening to others; sharing idea and having group discussions.
- Motivating yourself by asking "why" and seeking personal meaning.
- Learning through sensory input—moving, smelling, tasting.
- Hands-on learning by touching and using tools and objects.
- Keeping a journal to record feelings and spiritual values, not details.
- Studying with background music.
- Making up a rap song as a memory aid and to express feelings.
- Learning by teaching others; using people-oriented case studies.
- Playing with small children they way they want to play.

Characteristics of quadrant D thinking

Quadrant D thinking is visual, holistic, metaphorical, imaginative, creative, integrative, spatial, conceptual, flexible, and intuitive. It deals with futures, possibilities, synthesis, play, dreams, vision, strategic planning, the broader context, entrepreneurship, and change. A quadrant D culture is explorative, entrepreneurial, inventive, and future-oriented. It is playful, risk-driven, and independent. Pablo Picasso (modern painter), Leonardo da Vinci (Renaissance painter, sculptor, architect and scientist), Albert Einstein (physicist), and Amelia Earhart (aviation pioneer) are examples of strong quadrant D thinkers.

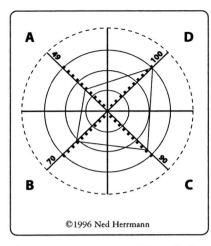

©1996 Ned Herrmann

***Figure 3.6** Typical average HBDI profile for female entrepreneurs (Ref. 3.3)*

Quadrant D thinkers enjoy design, art, architecture and geometry. Explorers and artists typically have strong quadrant D preferences, as do many scientists in R&D (engineering, medicine, physics). Quadrant D thinkers talk about "playing with an idea" or "the big picture" or "the cutting edge." Figure 3.6 depicts the typical average HBDI profile of female entrepreneurs—the comparable average for male entrepreneurs is A=71, B=60, C=65, D=90. Catalytic entrepreneurs typically would have quadrant D scores markedly higher than 100. Table 3.4 is a list of quadrant D learning activities.

***Table 3.4** Quadrant D Learning Activities and Behaviors*

- Looking for the big picture and context, not the details, of a topic.
- Doing simulations and asking what-if questions; brainstorming.
- Making use of visual aids; preferring pictures to words.
- Doing open-ended problems and finding several solutions.
- Experimenting and playing with ideas and possibilities.
- Thinking about the future; imagining different scenarios.
- Synthesizing ideas to come up with something new.
- Trying a different way (not the prescribed procedure) to do something, just for the fun of it.
- Making sketches to visualize a problem or solution; doodling.

Multidominant (whole-brain) thinking

We have just examined the characteristics of four distinct "ways of knowing." However, only 5 percent of people have a single strong dominance; 58 percent have a double dominance, 34 percent have a triple dominance, and only 3 percent have a profile with equal dominance in all four quadrants. Each person represents a unique coalition of thinking preferences. Imagine having a team of players inside your brain. You send out specialists for specific tasks; you send out one, two or maybe even three star players more often than the others, but to function well, the whole team is needed.

This is particularly true for the creative problem solving process. The successful generation, development and implementation of new ideas requires the systematic application of each of the four thinking styles. Whatever the particular pattern of thinking style dominance an individual possesses, it is possible to practice any of the four distinct styles when required and to do this effectively, given the kind of guidance and support this book is designed to provide. Although most people will

> *The brain is designed to be whole, but at the same time we can and must learn to appreciate our brain's uniqueness and that of others. A balanced view between wholeness and specialization is the key.*
>
> Ned Herrmann

naturally find certain thinking styles more comfortable than others, this should not be a surprise or a matter for concern when proceeding with the creative problem solving approach. The important point is to recognize and accept this virtually inevitable experience and avoid the temptation of rejecting those styles that come least naturally.

Many of these tensions and difficulties can be more easily overcome if the stages of the creative problem solving process are faced by a team rather than solo. In his work on whole brain thinking, Ned Herrmann placed considerable emphasis on its application to the more effective performance of teams. For our purposes here, two key points emerge:

1. Whole brain teams with all four thinking styles are more effective than teams where only one or two dominances are present. This is particularly significant where teams are self-selected since those with similar thinking styles tend to gravitate towards each other and thus may miss important viewpoints and problem solving strategies if they are not represented in the team's dominant thinking profile.

2. Equally important are the implications of the HBDI profile for communications. Tensions can arise within teams because of the different problem solving approaches taken by people with different brain dominance. Without an understanding of different thinking styles, the potential effectiveness of a team can be drastically reduced in practice because individuals with different styles communicate almost as if speaking different languages. Numerous examples exist where a raised awareness and appreciation of different thinking styles has greatly improved the functionality of teams within organizations and family groups—see Reference 3.1 for case studies. Communications barriers organized by thinking quadrant are listed in the activity on the facing page. For example, excessive chatter would annoy a quadrant A thinker, repetition a quadrant D thinker, and lack of closure a quadrant B thinker.

Activity 3.1: Barriers to Effective Communication (or What Can Drive People Crazy)

For good communication with a person with strong thinking preferences in a particular quadrant, avoid the barriers for that quadrant. In the list below, check the barriers that you think are making your communication with others less effective.

Barriers to communicating with Quadrant A thinkers:
- ☐ Inarticulate, "off the track" talking.
- ☐ Excessive chatter.
- ☐ Vague, ambiguous instructions.
- ☐ Illogical comments.
- ☐ Inefficient use of time.
- ☐ Lack of facts or data.
- ☐ Inappropriate informality.
- ☐ Overt sharing of personal feelings.
- ☐ Not knowing the "right" answer.
- ☐ Fear of challenge or debate.
- ☐ Lack of factual "proof" for ideas.
- ☐ Lack of clarity and precision.
- ☐ Excessive use of hands or gestures.
- ☐ Unrealistic touchy/feely approach.

Barriers to communicating with Quadrant B thinkers:
- ☐ Absence of clear agenda.
- ☐ Disorganized.
- ☐ Hopping from topic to topic.
- ☐ On and on and on and on.
- ☐ Unpredictable.
- ☐ Too fast paced.
- ☐ Unclear instructions or language.
- ☐ Too much beating around the bush.
- ☐ Incomplete sentences.
- ☐ Lack of closure.
- ☐ Not letting a person finish thinking.
- ☐ Lack of practicality.
- ☐ Too many ideas at once.
- ☐ Unexpected "off the wall" speech.

Barriers to communicating with Quadrant D thinkers:
- ☐ Repetition.
- ☐ Too slow paced.
- ☐ "Playing it safe" or "by the book."
- ☐ Overly structured, predictable.
- ☐ Absence of humor and fun.
- ☐ Lack of flexibility; too rigid.
- ☐ Not "getting" concepts/metaphors.
- ☐ Drowning in detail.
- ☐ Too many numbers.
- ☐ "Can't see the forest for the trees."
- ☐ Inability to talk about intangibles.
- ☐ Narrow focus.
- ☐ Resistance to new approaches.
- ☐ Dry, boring topic or style.

Barriers to communicating with Quadrant C thinkers:
- ☐ Lack of interaction.
- ☐ No eye contact.
- ☐ Impersonal approach or examples.
- ☐ Dry, stiff, or "cold" interaction.
- ☐ Insensitive comments.
- ☐ No time for personal sharing.
- ☐ Low recognition or praise.
- ☐ Lack of respect for feelings.
- ☐ Overly direct or brusque dialogue.
- ☐ Critical, judgmental attitude/voice.
- ☐ Being cut off or ignored.
- ☐ Lack of empathy for others.
- ☐ Avoidance of face-to-face meeting.
- ☐ All data, no nonsense.

Activity 3.2: Improve Your Communication

How do others see you? It can be helpful to ask others with whom you
have experienced communication challenges to go through the list of
communications barriers on the preceding page and indicate which traits
you have that form a barrier to effective communication with them, since
we are often unable to perceive these habits ourselves. Then pick two or
three items that you want to change. Make a plan with a supportive friend
or family member on how you can change your communication "flaws" and
how your progress will be monitored and encouraged over the next three
weeks. (Yes, it takes at least that long to change a habit.)

The Herrmann model and entrepreneurship

As we have seen in Chapter 2, an entrepreneur is a person who organizes and
manages a business and assumes the risk for the sake of profit. Adaptive
entrepreneurs are involved in businesses with comparatively low risk; they solve
problems in tried and understood ways by "doing things better." They manage
change incrementally, work within the system, and when collaborating
with inventors, supply stability, order, and organization. These people
actually implement inventions and thus institute innovation—the term from
entrepreneurship theory most closely associated with them is *allocating
entrepreneur*. Their strongest thinking preferences would tend to be in the left
brain quadrants A and B.

Inventive entrepreneurs "discover" problems and originate creative ideas and
creative solutions; they question assumptions and take risks; they do things
"differently." They provide strategic vision and create the dynamics to bring
about radical change. Thus they are *catalytic entrepreneurs* who originate breakthrough ideas. They are typically impatient with routine and detail and are seen
as chaotic and abrasive, with little respect for rules—all characteristics of
quadrant D thinkers. Inventive entrepreneurs need adaptive managers or team
members to help them implement their creative concepts and achieve innovation.

Figure 3.7 compares the Kirton model of adaptive/inventive thinking with the
definitions for entrepreneurs synthesized in Chapter 2. The Kirton scale is along
the horizontal axis and only indicates comparative degrees of preference for
adaptive or inventive thinking. Art Fry, the inventor of the Post-it notes, has
superimposed a bell-shaped curve to the Kirton scale to indicate a somewhat

quantitative measure on the different types of entrepreneurs, since only a comparatively few individuals would be found at the extreme range, and many are found in refining-type enterprises. According to Art Fry, CEOs and managers of established businesses typically want to keep the status quo and "do things the same way"—with little change. However, to remain competitive and survive in a changing environment, they are forced to either become adaptive or inventive to some degree to make their businesses more efficient.

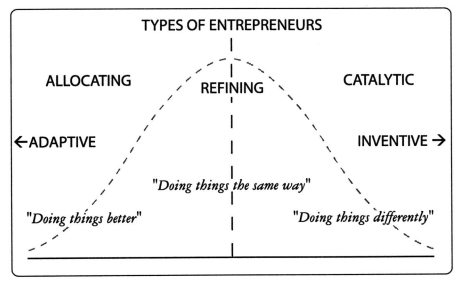

Figure 3.7 Different types of entrepreneurs and entrepreneurial managers

References for further learning

3.1 For case studies on HBDI applications, visit **www.hbdi.com**. Click on the library, then open the case studies and select any that may interest you. Also see the two entries under "Articles" and the separate summary of the *Harvard Business Review* article (Ref. 3.4).

3.2 Ned Herrmann, *The Creative Brain*, Herrmann International, Lake Lure, North Carolina, 1990. This "whole-brain" book explains the theory and development of the four-quadrant model of brain dominance and contains applications to many different areas of life.

3.3 Ned Herrmann, *The Whole Brain Business Book: Unlocking the Power of Whole Brain Thinking in Organizations and Individuals*, McGraw-Hill, New York, 1996. This book contains much insight and practical advice on how to use whole-brain thinking to enhance leadership, teamwork, and creativity in an organization to increase productivity.

3.4   Dorothy Leonard and Susaan Straus, "Putting Your Company's Whole Brain to Work," *Harvard Business Review Reprint 97407*, July-August 1997, pp. 110-121. It compares the HBDI with the MBTI and presents helpful hints on how to use team conflict constructively.

3.5   Edward Lumsdaine, Monika Lumsdaine, and J. William Shelnutt, *Creative Problem Solving and Engineering Design*, McGraw-Hill Primis, 1999, ISBN 0-07-236-0581-5. Chapters 3, 4, 5 (pp. 49-152) provide additional information, tools, exercises, and examples on the Herrmann model and applications to communications and teamwork.

When the intended communication is significant, it is necessary to design and deliver it in ways that allow for understanding to take place in all four quadrants.
My experience clearly demonstrates that the use of illustrations, graphics, stories, examples, and metaphors greatly enhances the likelihood that the intended meaning is conveyed to a wide range of people.

Ned Herrmann
The Whole Brain Business Book, p. 119

Exercises

Sales Ad Analysis: Obtain a selection of different sales advertisements for automobiles from magazines. Then in a heterogeneous group, select one and analyze what you like and dislike about the ad. How could the ad be improved by using all thinking quadrants?

Team Analysis: As a team, write up an analysis of your collective strengths and weaknesses. Which thinking preferences make it easy to communicate within the team? Which areas will need special attention in problem solving and executing your team project? Discuss how you can increase the mental diversity of your team.

Mission Statement: Obtain the mission statement of an organization you are associated with or know well. Look for clues in the vocabulary and "world view" for the dominant thinking quadrant(s). Is the mission statement in line with the day-to-day operation and values of the organization?

Whole-Brain Communications: Use a memo you have recently written or received. Do a "walk-around" (©1998 The Ned Herrmann Group) to identify areas where the memo could have been improved for better communication:

A: Does it use facts? Is it quantified? Does it show clear analysis? Is it to the point? Is it logical? Is the information complete?

B: Does it provide sufficient details? Does it give schedules? Is it in sequential order? Is it neat? Is it in an appropriate form? Was it checked for errors?

C: Does it use experiences that relate to the audience? Do personalized examples illustrate the point? Is it helpful and user-friendly? Does it acknowledge emotions?

D: Does it look at the big picture? Is it visual and colorful? Does it use metaphors? Does it look to the future? Is it conceptually sound? Does it address risk and change issues?

Turn-On Work: In Table 3.5, circle the eight elements that most turn you on. Turn-on items are usually strongly aligned with your thinking preferences. Underline the two elements that turn you off the most. These are usually found in the diagonally opposite quadrant of your strongest preference. This analysis is more difficult to do when your thinking preferences are evenly distributed over all four quadrants. Only the HBDI can give an accurate indication of your thinking preferences.

Table 3.5 *Turn-On Work Exercise (from Ref. 3.3, p. 26)*

A	**D**
Working solo	Taking risks
Analyzing data	Providing vision
Applying formulas	Strategic planning
Logical processing	Seeing the big picture
Making a critical judgment	Bringing about change
Dealing with technical stuff	Playing around and experimenting
Dealing with numbers and hardware	Inventing solutions and alternatives
Making (*or knowing how*) things work	Designing & developing new things
Having structure & proper sequence	Getting groups to work well together
Having an ordered environment	Helping and encouraging people
Dealing with forms and files	Expressing ideas and feelings
Planning things out in detail	Teaching, training, coaching
Getting things done on time	Listening and talking
Preserving the status quo	Building networks
Being in control	Communicating
B Organizing	Counseling **C**

> *Entrepreneurship is the process of identifying, developing, and bringing a vision to life. The vision may be an innovative idea, an opportunity, or simply a better way to do something. The end result of this process is the creation of a new venture, formed under conditions of risk and considerable uncertainty.*
>
> Entrepreneurship Center at Miami University in Ohio

Four-Quadrant Analysis of Entrepreneurship Definition: From what you have learned about the four different thinking styles and "clues" in the Herrmann model, do a proforma analysis of the boxed definition above. How many words or phrases are clues to a specific thinking preference? How balanced is the definition between left-brain and right-brain thinking? Which thinking quadrants are addressed? _____

_____

_____

_____

_____

_____

_____

_____

_____

Action checklist

➤ Do you and the people you work or study with understand the Herrmann model and the power of the HBDI? Do they understand and appreciate their own thinking preferences and that of others?

➤ Does your communication address all four thinking quadrants? Analyze a recent presentation you made for a general audience to gauge your strong and weak points.

➤ Identify people with whom you have frequent interactions—the people who are most important to you. What are their strongest thinking preferences (based on your understanding of the Herrmann model and the "clues" in their behavior)? To which quadrants might you be "deaf" or "blind" unless you pay special attention?

Chapter 4
The Creative Problem Solving Model

This chapter presents an overview of the creative problem solving model and associated metaphorical mindsets, followed by a more detailed discussion of each step and some of the tools available to accomplish the tasks and objectives. But before we begin, we will briefly survey some commonly used problem solving approaches.

Common problem solving schemes

A problem is not only something that is not working right or an assignment teachers give to students—a problem is anything that could be fixed or improved through some change. A problem is finding the best birthday gift ever for someone you love. A problem is inventing something (a product or service) that fills a specific need. Schools heavily emphasize the teaching of analytical problem solving methods. Yet it has been estimated that about eighty percent of all problems in life need to be approached with creative thinking.

Table 4.1 compares problem-solving approaches that are taught in various fields. In addition to these methods, some people may use unguided experimentation, trial and error, or guessing—these commonly have unreliable outcomes and are not included here. Creative problem solving is a structured model that uses exploratory, analytical, creative, critical, organized and interpersonal thinking in the most effective sequence to obtain optimum outcomes. Effective problem solving is applying this whole-brain model iteratively to achieve a desired goal, such as starting a successful business enterprise (as will be shown in Part 2 of this book).

> People have always had distinct preferences in their approaches to problem solving.
> Today's pace of change demands that these individuals quickly develop the ability to work together.
> Rightly harnessed, the energy released by the intersection of different thought processes will propel innovation.
>
> Dorothy Leonard and Susaan Straus
> (Ref. 3.4)

Table 4.1 *Problem Solving Schemes of Various Fields*

Method	Phase 1	Phase 2	Phase 3	Phase 4
Science Scientific method	Inductive data analysis and hypothesis.	Deduce possible solutions.	Test alternate solutions.	Implement best solution.
Psychology Creative thinking	Exploration of resources.	Incubation – possibilities.	Illumination – definite decision on solution.	Verification and modifications.
Math Polya's method	What is the problem?	Plan the solution.	Look at alternatives.	Carry out the plan; check the results.
Engineering Analytical thinking	Define and sketch system; identify unknowns.	Model the problem.	Conduct analysis and experiments.	Evaluate the final results.
Industry Team problem solving	1. Use a team approach. 2. Collect data; define the problem.	3. Deal with emergencies. 4. Find the root cause.	5. Test corrective action; devise action plan. 6. Implement plan.	7. Prevent problem recurrence. 8. Congratulate team.
Many Areas Creative problem solving	1. Define the problem. Explore the context; analyze data.	2. Generate many ideas. 3. Synthesize better ideas.	4. Judge the ideas; decide on best solution.	5. Implement the solution; do a follow-up. What have you learned?

The field-specific problem solving schemes in Table 4.1 have limitations. The *scientific method* is taught and reported as a sequential procedure, whereas the actual process includes many detours—with intuition and idea synthesis—that are rarely recognized and acknowledged. *Creative thinking* adopts the first idea that comes to mind and may not necessarily lead to a superior solution, since better alternatives are not sought. *Analytical problem solving* is taught well in mathematics and engineering courses but cannot be applied to other types of problems because it discourages contextual, holistic, and intuitive thinking. Large companies have developed their own problem solving methods based on a *team approach*, but because few people on these teams have training in creative thinking, analytical thinking predominates and innovative design concepts or solutions are rare.

Creative problem solving as outlined in Figure 4.1 can be effectively used in all but routine problems. It will prevent superficial solutions to deep-seated operational and strategic problems and long-term solutions to short-term tactical problems. It is a key for addressing unstructured, elusive, ambiguous problems. Creative problem solving has five steps that are specifically related to six different metaphorical mindsets with distinct ways of thinking as shown superimposed on the Herrmann model in Figure 4.2 in the following section. Each mindset is like an open tool box, with many different techniques available to enhance the thinking and problem solving process to achieve an optimum result, depending on the type, goals and context of the problem, the time and resources available, the experiences and training of the team members, and the organizational culture.

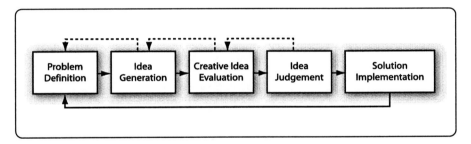

Figure 4.1 *The iterative creative problem solving process*

We first learned about different problem-solving mindsets from Roger Von Oech (Ref. 4.1). We added the "detective" for data analysis to the "explorer" to indicate that both left-brain and right-brain thinking are required for complete problem definition. To emphasize a key step in creative problem solving—idea synthesis and optimization—we invented the "engineer." This mindset is placed between the right-brain "artist" and the left-brain "judge" and iterates rapidly between creative and analytical thinking. And we changed the "warrior" into the "producer" in response to requests from students and teachers for a more positive image. These metaphors make it easier to remember the type of thinking that we need to use at each creative problem-solving step.

Steps and associated metaphors in creative problem solving

1. Problem Definition

When we look at the big picture or context of a problem or want to discover its opportunity and future-oriented aspects, we use the mindset of an EXPLORER, primarily using thinking quadrants C and D. To find the root causes of problems, we need to think like a DETECTIVE looking for clues and asking questions, primarily using thinking quadrants A and B. Problem definition culminates in a positive problem definition statement based on an analysis of the collected information.

2. Idea Generation

Here we brainstorm a multitude of creative ideas based on the problem definition in the imaginative, intuitive mindset of an ARTIST, using thinking quadrants C and D.

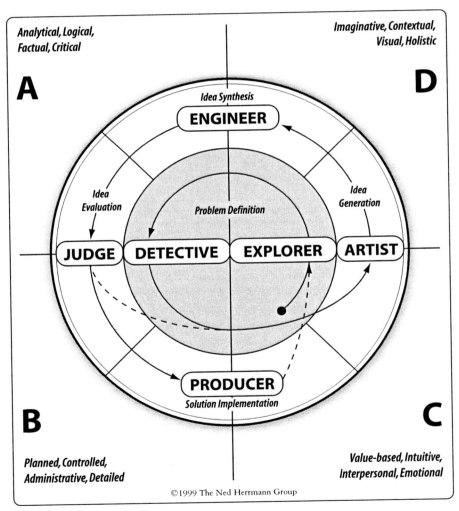

Figure 4.2 *How creative problem solving relates to the Herrmann model*

3. Idea Synthesis

In the creative idea evaluation phase, we play around with the brainstormed ideas to obtain fewer but more practical, optimized, synthesized solutions using the mindset of an ENGINEER in thinking quadrants D and A.

4. Idea Judgment

In the *critical* idea evaluation phase, we must determine which ideas and solutions are best and should be implemented, in the mindset of a JUDGE and primarily using thinking quadrants A and B.

5. Solution Implementation

Putting a solution into action requires a new round of creative problem solving in the mindset of the PRODUCER. The focus is primarily on quadrant C communication and on quadrant B planning to carry the project to a successful conclusion.

Let's play with the six mindsets and look at some common problem-solving scenarios:

- What would happen if we left out the "explorer" or "detective"? We can still come up with ideas and find a solution, except that the solution may not solve the real problem.

- What would happen if we left out the "artist" and "engineer"? This happens when we take the first idea that comes to mind and rush to implement it without looking for alternatives. It happens when the "judge" appears too soon in the process—when we tell ourselves, "This is a dumb idea" or ridicule the creative ideas of others. Most analytical problem solving approaches skip these two mindsets.

- What happens when we leave out the "judge"? Without the "judge," we will not be able to select the best idea or find and correct the flaws of ideas.

- What would happen if we only had the "producer"? This might work in rare cases, when a solution out of the blue actually works by sheer luck. But to create conditions for developing an optimum solution to a problem, it is best to follow the process in the most effective sequence, whether we work alone or in a team.

As we have seen in Chapter 3, we can expect better solutions if we use all four brain quadrants or thinking styles. The brain has the strongest connections between the cerebral and limbic halves; thus we can most easily switch between quadrant A and quadrant B thinking or quadrant C and quadrant D thinking. Alternating quickly between quadrants A and D or quadrants B and C can be learned and becomes easier with practice, since the two brain halves are connected with special fibers. However, switching between diagonally opposite quadrants is difficult and takes longer because there are no direct connections in the brain between these quadrants (see Figure 3.1). Thus the brain has to "translate" via an intermediate quadrant to achieve a switch. The creative problem solving model has these intermediate steps built in.

But why are the iterative cycles in a counter-clockwise direction? When we analyzed the *knowledge-creation* cycle developed by Nonaka and Takeuchi (Ref. 2.4) in terms of the Herrmann model, we found that it moved from Step 1— quadrant C *motivation* (through personal experiences, customer interface, shared beliefs and values in a team) to Step 2—quadrant D *vision* (through metaphors, models, new concepts, brainstorming and divergent thinking) to Step 3—quadrant A *information* flow and explicit systemic knowledge (through context-specific data collection, analysis, documentation, and dissemination) to Step 4—quadrant B *implementation* to solve problems and do the job well (which involves mastery "learning by doing," prototyping or piloting new products or processes, and on-the-job training to gain tacit operational knowledge). The sequence of creative problem solving mindsets corresponds to the knowledge creation model (which spirals through the four steps from the individual to the team and then the organizational level (see pages 67-79 in Ref. 3.5 for a more detailed explanation).

Problem definition

Overview and objectives

A problem has two aspects—danger and opportunity—although one may be more apparent than the other. It is easy to overlook the opportunity aspect when dealing with an emergency. Yet once the crisis has been dealt with, we can introduce a policy of continuous improvement or creatively make a fundamental change leading to innovation. The two aspects of

Wei ji.
The Chinese symbol for crisis is made up of two words:
danger + opportunity

problem definition require two different mindsets: the "detective" to address the crisis and the "explorer" to exploit the opportunity, as contrasted in Table 4.2. To identify the real problem and its context, we need to use the whole brain.

Table 4.2 *Whole-Brain Problem Definition*

Type of problem

Detective: Assigned a problem or crisis. Something is not working right.

Explorer: Finding or identifying a "mess." Discovering a problem, need or opportunity.

People involved

Detective: Autocratic chain-of-command. Who is responsible? Who is the expert?

Explorer: Cooperative teamwork; include people from other fields, not experts.

Viewpoint and scope

Detective: What is terrible about a particular situation? Narrow scope, with focus on task.

Explorer: What would be nice if it could be done? Systems thinking; explore change.

Information

Detective: List known facts. Determine what data are needed. Look for causes/clues.

Explorer: Look into context and trends; set goals. Imagine the future or ideal situation.

Boundaries

Detective: Determine constraints and limits on time, budget, staff, and resources.

Explorer: Keep limits in the back of the mind; seek to overcome the boundaries.

Problem solving paradigm

Detective: Use existing tools and methods. Traditional, analytical, convergent thinking.

Explorer: Look for new approaches or alternatives. Divergent, intuitive, flexible thinking.

Example: A group of middle-school students wanted to creatively solve the problem of bicycle theft. As "detectives" they tested chain and cable type locks with hacksaws and bolt cutters. A customer survey, to their surprise, found that the biggest problem with bike locks was that owners could not open them because they forgot the combination. The "explorers" saw the larger picture and changed the *real* problem to bike security, where bike design, parking, and registration schemes would be included in potential solutions and where the solution might be applied to other uses.

The "explorer" for divergent thinking

The main objective of "explorers" is to discover the larger context of a problem, as symbolically illustrated in Figuree 4.3. They must have a sense of adventure and an eye for the far view. "Explorers" use quadrant D thinking to speculate

about possibilities, opportunities, and futures that may be connected to the problem. And they use quadrant C thinking modes to investigate how the problem impacts people. The explorer's mindset provides a divergent, positive, long-term perspective to balance the more narrowly focused, convergent, and often negative thinking of the "detective"—the sheer amount of data collected by "detectives" may make the problem look overwhelming.

Figure 4.3 The explorer's mindset

Trend watching, or how to anticipate the future

Studying trends can help us see the development of problems in a wider context and time frame. With this information, we may be better able to devise appropriate solutions. Studying trends lets us identify actions, markets, and future products or services—it is a valuable skill for inventors and innovators. In an article on "How to Think Like an Innovator" in the May-June 1988 issue of *The Futurist*

> *Where the telescope ends, the microscope begins. Which of the two has the grander view?*
>
> Victor Hugo, *Les Misérables*

magazine, Denis E. Waitley and Robert B. Tucker, two California consultants on personal and executive development, offer some ideas on how to become a good trend watcher, as summarized in Table 4.3.

Table 4.3 Tips on How to Become a Good Trend Spotter

Audit your information intake; make your reading time count!
Cut down on mental "junk" food—make informed choices about what you currently read. Innovators may spend as much as a third of their day reading. Read articles that contain ideas; take notes as you read. Look for what is different, incongruous, worrisome, exciting, unexpected. Seek to broaden your world view. Look for developing trends.

Develop your front-line observational skills; ask questions!
Become a people watcher. Listen in on conversations to find out how people think and feel. How do the main topics of conversation change over time? What perspectives do you pick up from the popular culture (movies, MTV, chat rooms)? Ask questions in all kinds of situations—how else can you really know what the customer wants?

Find opportunities!
Search for solutions to negative trends and offer a means of prevention. Watch for patterns that can tip you off to new opportunities. Even when a present trend is against you, it can be used to come up with a breakthrough idea to counteract it. Also, watch what the competition is doing and do it better, with added value.

Other tools and techniques for "explorers"

In addition to observing trends, "explorers" can use a number of tools for problem exploration, from the personal, introspective level to group brainstorming activities such as *Synectics* (Ref. 4.5) and *Morphological Creativity* (Ref. 4.7)—both advanced techniques that require training. Or they can network with experts in the problem area and its context. As an entrepreneur, you will benefit from using the following resources:

1. **Searching the Web.** Use the search engine capabilities of the Internet to surf for information, not just in the specific problem area but also at its fringes and related areas. If you are inventing or improving a product, it is crucial that you conduct a preliminary patent search. Instructions for doing patent searches are given in Part 2, Chapter 6 of this book.

2. **Enhancing Your Intuitive Insight.** Alone or in a team, try to model the problem using a wide range of artistic materials and props. Or play the "Don't sell me game" (given in Part 2, Section 6) or any other brainstorming activity where non-judgmental thinking is encouraged.

3. **Mind Mapping.** This technique combines aspects of brainstorming, sketching, and diagramming in the process of thinking through a subject and organizing the available information. Tony Buzan, a British brain researcher, invented this method in the 1970s. It was originally developed as a note-taking technique that can display the relationships between facts and ideas. Computer programs such as *MindManager 2002* or *Inspiration* can do mind mapping. Reference 4.9 gives some interesting web sites with directions and illustrations on how to do mind mapping.

The "detective" for convergent thinking

"Detectives" deal with crisis and danger—their job is to look for the root causes of problems. They do not assume that they already know what the *real* problem is. Therefore, they look for information that is hidden. To find it, they must be persistent; they must think logically about where and how to find the desired

detailed information and clues; they must use the right "lenses" as illustrated in Figure 4.4. A methodical, careful quadrant B approach combined with quadrant A analytical thinking is needed. Agents in the FBI and the people from the CDC (Centers for Disease Control in Atlanta, Georgia) who were working on tracking down the trail of the anthrax infection during the fall of 2001 in the US used "detective" tools to find information and identify the sources of the contamination.

Figure 4.4 *The dectective's mindset*

Tools and techniques for "detectives"

"Detectives" have a virtual toolbox of techniques available that can help in identifying the root causes of problems. The choice is guided by the type of problem, the organization's problem-solving culture, and the available time, budget, and expertise. Special training is usually needed to learn to use the specialized analytical tools.

1. **Asking questions (Kepner-Tregoe approach).** Detectives ask questions about who, what, where, when, why, and how much. Long lists of questions

have been published to help in this process of data collection. In the Kepner-Tregoe method, the problem is defined as the extent of change from a former satisfactory state to the present unsatisfactory state, and finding the causes of the deviation should help solve the problem. It also helps to describe the problem in terms of what it is *not* (Ref. 4.3).

2. **Surveys.** Manufacturing and service companies depend on surveys to collect data on "the voice of the customer." When this data is analyzed (and visualized with a Pareto diagram), it often yields insight into the real problem that is surprisingly different from the original perception and can change the direction of problem solving.

3. **Introspection.** When time is too short to do in-depth data collection and analysis, we can engage in a few minutes of quiet introspection. We dig into our memories to bring up and share any information that we already have about the problem, before the team collectively works out a problem definition statement.

4. **Statistical process control (SPC).** Manufacturing companies frequently use SPC, which includes seven different tools: check sheets, histograms, cause-and-effect (fishbone) diagrams, Pareto diagrams, scatter diagrams, process control charts, and additional documentation. These are methods for finding the causes of problems by making graphs of the data and then analyzing the results.

5. **Force field analysis.** The problem is analyzed in terms of supporting and hindering forces and their strengths on the way toward achieving a satisfactory state or solution.

6. **Other methods.** Ford Motor Company, for example, uses two specific methods to analyze causes of failures. *Failure mode and effects analysis (FMEA)* explores all possible failure modes for a product or a process, and *fault tree analysis (FTA)* is restricted to the identification of the system elements and events that could lead to or have led to a single, particular failure. The following specialized

> *The form of made things is always subject to change in response to their real or perceived shortcomings, their failure to function properly. This principle governs invention, innovation, and ingenuity; it is what drives all inventors, innovators, and engineers.*
>
> Henry Petroski,
> *The Evolution of Useful Things*

methods for "detectives" are very challenging and time consuming. Carefully *designed experiments based on statistical methods* are conducted to get the data needed to answer the list of questions and define the problem accurately. In *Weibull analysis*, the results of testing products to failure are plotted on a log-log paper. When warranty claims about a product need to be analyzed, or products and services are evaluated against the competition, *benchmarking techniques* are employed. *Quality function deployment (QFD)* is used to improve the quality of a product's components above that of the best competing product.

How to complete the problem definition phase

Detectives are responsible for bringing problem definition to a close by completing four tasks: assessing available resources, writing the briefing document, stating the problem definition, and collecting solution ideas popping up during the incubation period.

1. **Resource assessment.** Consider the following relevant factors: Is the problem an emergency? How much time is available for problem solving? Who is available to help you solve the problem, as a team member or expert? What about finances? What is your budget for the problem solving process and for implementing the solution? If no money is available, you must either concentrate on ways that do not cost much or include fund raising as a separate problem.

2. **Briefing document.** Whether a team or individual is involved in problem solving or when a paper trail or documentation is required or desirable, the information collected about the problem should be assembled in a briefing document (see Table 4.4) for distribution to the problem-solving team or other stakeholders. Although the data collection file may be substantial, the briefing document should be brief—at most a page or two for all but very complex problems.

Table 4.4 *Contents of the Briefing Document*

1. Background and context of the problem, including trends.
2. Specific data collected about the problem, with data analysis.
3. Summary of things that were tried but did not work.
4. Thoughts on possible solutions that have come to mind (attached).
5. Conclusion: What is the real problem?
6. The problem definition statement expressed as a positive goal.

3. **Problem definition statement.** This statement, in positive terms, will direct your thoughts or the thoughts of the brainstorming team toward solutions. This goal can be quite specific or an "impossible" big dream. "How can we serve our customers better" most likely will result in mundane ideas, but "How can we provide instant service" will force the mind to seek unusual or innovative ways to reach the goal. Play around with several versions of the statement before selecting the best one; use a thesaurus to find synonyms. If a team is involved, brief the members ahead of the scheduled brainstorming. Team members can ask questions and share insight to make sure they understand the problem and the solution goals.

Example: Improving a Problem Definition Statement

a. *"Secondary school students have a hard time understanding the concept of centripetal force."*
   This definition puts the spotlight on the problem and is thus not a positive statement looking to solutions.

b. *"Design a mini merry-go-round that will let students experience centripetal force."*
   This definition is too narrowly focused on a particular solution. The idea should be jotted down, however, as a possible solution to start the brainstorming, but the definition needs to be broader.

c. *"Teachers need an inexpensive device (presently unavailable) to use in the classroom to enable student to experience and experiment with rotational motion and the forces involved."*
   This definition invites other solutions (besides a merry-go-round) that might solve the problem; also, it provides some criteria.

---

4. **Incubation and collective notebook.** The mind needs "soak time" so it will be prepared to generate innovative ideas. An overnight period makes a good time-out, or a week may be most convenient in your schedule. At the least, organize a refreshment break with some relaxing activities. Both Albert Einstein and Thomas Edison played a musical instrument or went for a walk when they needed creative ideas. During this incubation, all solution ideas that come to mind must be quickly jotted down, or they will be forgotten. Our mind often has to be cleared of the well-known solutions before we can come up with truly novel ideas. The notes are collected and a summary of the results is prepared, with the most interesting ideas used for further exploration or to start the brainstorming session in the next creative problem solving stage.

Idea generation

Visualize being in a thunderstorm. You see and feel the awesome power of wind and lightning. Wouldn't it be wonderful if this energy could be harnessed and put to good use? In a way, when we brainstorm, we want to provoke a storm of ideas. A gentle breeze just won't have the same result. Brainstorming procedures are like a harness for directing and optimizing the energy in idea generation. We will first present classic brainstorming and then summarize some variations that have been developed to accommodate special conditions. Brainstorming can be done by individuals (especially when using a more "graphical" method such as mind mapping). However, an effort should be made when dealing with complex problems to bring at least a small team together for this stage to increase the possibility that novel ideas will be generated, usually by people not too personally involved with the problem.

The verbal method known as classic brainstorming was developed in 1938 by Alex Osborn in his advertising business. It then came into widespread use in the 1950's as a group method of creative idea generation. The best number of people

for verbal brainstorming is from three to ten. Brainstorming does not work for all types of problems all the time, but its successes have made it a valuable problem-solving tool. It is easy to learn, and it gets more productive with practice. People frequently mistake random, routine, critical discussion in meetings as brainstorming. As you will see, brainstorming requires careful mental preparation. Although it is a creative, freewheeling activity, definite rules and procedures are followed.

Figure 4.5 *The artist's mindset*

The role of the "artist"

Generating and igniting imaginative ideas is at the heart of the creative problem-solving process—and the mindset required is shown in Figure 4.5. Artists create something new, something that first existed only in their minds. As artists, our task in creative problem solving is to transform information into new ideas. We can and must break out of our usual mold—we can go to town with our quadrant D imagination and our quadrant C feelings! Welcome eccentric, wild, weird, crazy, off-the-wall, out-of-the-box ideas and "fireworks"— your own or those of your team! In brainstorming, this mental activity of using the imagination is called "freewheeling." This means we impose few restrictions on ourselves or our team members on the types of ideas that can be expressed.

The four rules of brainstorming

Brainstorming is easy to learn because it only has four rules. These four rules are important principles, so fix them firmly in your mind!

1. Generate as many solutions as possible—quantity counts.
2. Wild ideas are welcome—be as creative as you can be.
3. "Hitchhiking" is encouraged—build on the ideas of others.
4. No criticism is allowed—defer judgment until the evaluation phase.

The more ideas you generate, the better the chance that you will come up with an innovative solution. The wilder the ideas, the greater the odds of generating a truly original concept! The only boundary here is to avoid words and ideas that are hurtful or offensive to your team members because the stress that is caused will inhibit creative thinking and undermine the team spirit. Ideas do not have to be completely new—you are encouraged to hitchhike on other people's ideas. Idea pinching is allowed! Do not put down ideas or the people who express them (including yourself). Humor, laughter, and applause are valued responses. In brainstorming, there are no dumb ideas or wrong answers. These rules must be observed no matter which brainstorming technique is used or how many people participate (and even if you brainstorm solo).

Freedom versus control

Strongly left-brain thinkers may feel uncomfortable with sharing ideas involving quadrant C emotions or "impractical" quadrant D thinking. If you have such reactions, give yourself explicit permission to play and express all kinds of ideas. Brainstorming is fun! Be surprised by the freedom of the "storm." The interaction that occurs between the minds of collaborating team members is important; ideas can be used as igniters or stepping-stones to new ideas, or they can be combined or synthesized in new and unexpected ways. Wild ideas are valuable and needed at this stage—the normal forces of life will make them more practical later. Maintaining a safe, uncritical climate for expressing creative ideas is important here because these ideas can be very fragile.

Strongly right-brained people may find it difficult to follow "rules." Procedures can ensure that brainstorming will be as efficient and productive as possible. Constraints can both help and hinder brainstorming. They attempt to contain the "storm" within a specific goal or problem area. If they are too rigid, a vigorous "storm" cannot develop. But a limited number of carefully thought-out constraints will not significantly affect creativity. The problem definition statement is a useful constraint: it provides direction and a target for idea generation, as well as boundaries. However, team members should also have permission to push the boundaries—this is when breakthrough ideas may appear.

Procedure for leading a verbal brainstorming session

The step-by-step procedure for conducting a brainstorming session is presented from the facilitator's point of view, with the preparations summarized in Table 4.5. Since you are now learning about brainstorming, it is likely that you will be leading sessions in the future.

Table 4.5 *Preparation for Verbal Brainstorming*

Team members: Stakeholders affected by the problem and solution should be among the brainstorming team, and some members should have quadrant D thinking preferences. All should receive the briefing document ahead of the brainstorming session if possible.

Location: People are able to think more creatively if they are in an unfamiliar location. Thus, find a place with beautiful, relaxing surroundings. At the least, select a room that is "different"—not one regularly used for meetings. Seat people in a circle or horse-shoe. If you must use a conference room with a long table and facing chairs, enhance the atmosphere with classical background music, colored posters, and a fragrant snack.

Schedule: Brainstorming is exhausting; thus do not plan to cover more than two topics or exceed a three-hour period. Pick a time and day that shields people from the stress of pressing business.

Materials: Obtain and set up the necessary equipment: easels, flip charts, markers, note cards, and visual aids or props to stimulate creative thinking. For long sessions, have light refreshments, including coffee or tea. A tape recorder can capture comments that do not get written down during the session. For a large team, an assistant can help write down ideas.

Step 1 – Briefing. Give the team members a few minutes for social interaction and for comfortably seating themselves. Turn on the tape recorder and open with a review of the briefing, inviting team members to share any insight that came to mind during incubation. Jot down solution ideas on a flip chart. Prominently post the problem definition statement; amend it if desired. Make sure that distractions on people's minds or in the room's environment are taken care of before the actual brainstorming starts.

Step 2 – Review the rules and required mindset. Review the four brainstorming rules. Explain that anyone offering more than two negative remarks will be asked to leave the session—this is the "three strikes and you're out" policy for preventing a negative atmosphere. Review the characteristics of the artist's mindset to be used for the brainstorming session.

Step 3 – Explain the procedure. Explain that all ideas and combinations of ideas will be numbered and recorded. In a small team, ideas can be called out as fast as they can be written down on the flip chart. In large teams, members have to take turns speaking. The other participants must jot

> *Problems cannot be solved by thinking within the framework in which the problems were created.*
> Albert Einstein

down all ideas that flash into their minds, so they won't forget them while they await their turn. Ask for brief statements only; the "engineer" will have an opportunity later for elaboration. Set an initial time limit of 20-30 minutes. Adding a quota is often helpful to increase the number of ideas generated, such as, "Let's see if we can come up with 50 ideas in 20 minutes."

Step 4 – Warm-up exercise. Conduct a 5-minute warm-up in creative thinking using a simple, familiar object (brick, pencil, popped corn, ruler, coffee cup, floppy disk or CD). Turn on the classical background music now to encourage right-brain thinking modes. Jot down the called-out ideas on a flip chart. Usually, mundane ideas will be expressed at first. When more humorous ideas come forth and the team members relax with laughter, their minds are "primed" and you can start to brainstorm the defined problem. An example (using a square of aluminum foil for a warm-up) is given in Chapter 7.

Step 5 – Brainstorming. Teams usually begin by dumping out obvious, well-known ideas—these have to be purged from the mind before it can bring out really new, creative ideas. Write down all ideas; when a sheet is full, post it on the wall. If the flow of ideas is very slow or stuck, encourage the process by throwing out a wild idea to serve as a stepping-stone (or use some other appropriate technique). But don't rush into this; quiet periods to allow reflection and synthesis in the subconscious mind can be beneficial.

Step 6 – Close. Once the flow of ideas has slowed down to a trickle and the announced time is up, give an extra three minutes. Some of the best ideas are often generated during this time. Or challenge the team to come up with 5-10 additional ideas before stopping.

Step 7 – Dismissal. Thank the team members for their participation and let them know what will happen next. Collect all ideas that were written down, as well as the tape recording, for later processing and evaluation. Encourage the team members to e-mail you additional ideas that might come to them in the next few days.

Other brainstorming methods

What if you have shy or domineering team members? What if you have a group of 100 or more people you want to involve in brainstorming? What if there is open conflict among people who must participate? To address special circumstances, other brainstorming techniques have been developed—a few of the easier, low-tech approaches are compiled in Table 4.6. Table 4.7 lists techniques that can be used to get idea generation going. Many books are available for

> *Many ideas grow better when transplanted into another mind than in the one where they sprang up.*
> Oliver Wendell Holmes

information on alternate brainstorming methods (for example, Ref. 4.7). TRIZ (Ref. 2.7), Morphological Creativity, and Synectics are very complicated and require special training and a basic knowledge of science in the case of TRIZ.

High-tech (electronic) brainstorming

Computers can be used for brainstorming, and a number of software packages are available. *IdeaFisher* is probably one of the best known and has survived the test of time. Computer programs can inject out-of-the-box ideas and are thus beneficial when a homogeneous workgroup is brainstorming—especially a group that is stuck in routine problem-solving habits. In this case, only one computer is required. Similarly, the program can also enhance brainstorming by individuals. If everyone on the team has access to a networked computer, the members can brainstorm from their own desks in a "virtual" meeting. Research seems to indicate that the productivity (quantity as well as quality) of ideas generated by electronic brainstorming is not significantly different from that

Table 4.6 *Some Simple Brainstorming Methods*

1. Pin card method: written technique for a small group of shy or confrontational people.
2. Crawford slip writing: for large groups, with each person submitting 20 – 30 ideas.
3. "Ringgi" process: People sequentially modify a proposed idea; this avoids conflict.
4. Panel method: 7 volunteers out of 30 – 40 people brainstorm; all others jot down ideas, which are then collected for later evaluation.
5. Story board: Ideas are brainstormed, written on note cards, and posted under different categories on a wall or large board.
6. Electronic brainstorming/bulletin board: Ideas are collected on a posted problem.
7. Idea trigger: Individual lists are shared in a group and trigger additional creative ideas.
8. Gallery method: people work on individual flip charts; inspect each other's ideas; add modifications.
9. Mind mapping: "visual" method especially useful for individual brainstorming.

Table 4.7 *What to Do When You Are "Stuck"*

1. Imagine success: Imagine the ideal situation; mentally remove all constraints.
2. Imagine the worst: Imagine the most absurd things to do to solve the problem.
3. Force-fitting ideas: Force two wild, unrelated ideas together to generate solutions; purposefully search for wild options.
4. Free association: Start this "game" with a symbol; continue a chain to good ideas.
5. Big dream: Think of a fantastic dream solution and wishful scenarios; play a "what if" game.
6. Thought-starter tools: Osborn's Nine Questions and commercial tools based on the nine (or similar) questions.
7. Attribute listing and sequence-attribute/modifications matrix (SAMM).
8. Bionics: Ask, "How is the problem solved in nature?"
9. The force-fit game: Two teams pose crazy questions and find good applications.

obtained by traditional techniques, although there are indications that idea generation by computer (if it can be done anonymously) may be less inhibiting for some individuals who lack the self-confidence for sharing wild ideas in a group.

Creative idea evaluation

Idea evaluation is a two-step process, where each step uses a different mindset. First comes creative idea evaluation in the engineer's mindset, followed by critical evaluation in the judge's mindset. The two steps are used iteratively in the Pugh method, a structured process of creative concept evaluation for synthesizing an optimum solution described in detail in Chapter 5.

The role of the "engineer" in creative idea evaluation

Creative idea evaluation is basically a second, focused round of brainstorming that builds on the ideas generated the first time around. The required mindset is symbolized in Figure 4.6. The goal is to arrive at practical ideas that have

the potential for solving the original problem. What do "engineers" do? They categorize, combine, and develop the "artist's" ideas; they synthesize, force-fit, and generate additional creative ideas. Also, each wild idea is questioned: How can it be used as a stepping stone to a better idea? What is useful or valuable about this? Can it be improved? "Engineers" move quickly between quadrant D and quadrant A thinking while keeping a nonjudgmental, positive attitude.

Figure 4.6 *The engineer's mindset*

The four rules of creative idea evaluation

Like brainstorming, creative idea evaluation also has four rules.

1. Look for quality and "better" ideas.
2. Make wild ideas more practical.
3. Synthesize ideas to obtain more complete, optimized solutions.
4. Maintain a positive attitude; continue to defer critical judgment.

Instead of quantity, we are now aiming for quality. Look for the good in each idea and try to make it even better. Use wild ideas as stepping-stones or thought-starters to generate more practical solutions. This requires iteration between creative and analytical thinking. Instead of hitchhiking on ideas, we will now try to integrate, synthesize, force-fit, or meld different ideas to develop optimal solutions. We will continue to abstain from quick judgments and negative comments; instead, we try to overcome obvious flaws in ideas with additional creative thinking.

Timing and preparation

If possible, wait at least one day after the original brainstorming—creative idea evaluation will be more productive if done with fresh minds. This time lag will also give the facilitator, team leader, or the entire team a chance to do some preliminary organizing work with the pool of brainstormed ideas.

To prepare for idea evaluation, each brainstormed idea is written on a separate note card. Some teams may prefer to use Post-it notes instead. Use a heavy pen and print legibly; start writing at the top of the card to leave some blank space for notes at the bottom, and include the identification number. When new ideas come to mind during this process (as is quite likely), they are written down on cards, too, and added to the stack.

The facilitator needs to bring the following materials to the evaluation session: the completed idea cards, blank cards, pens in different colors for writing on the cards, paper clips, rubber bands, a flip chart, markers, and masking tape, pins or tacks. The meeting room should have a large table, with additional work areas and empty wall space where flip chart pages (or the Post-it notes) can be posted. If the time available for idea evaluation is short, the facilitator can do Task 1 ahead of time. Keep in mind that creative evaluation may take two or three times as long as the original brainstorming.

The creative idea evaluation process

This is an open-ended activity involving brainstorming—thus the results are not very predictable, even though a structured, three-step approach is used.

TASK 1 – Sorting related ideas into categories

The idea cards are randomly spread out over the table. Ponder the ideas in silence for a few minutes, either as an individual or with the entire team gathered around the table. Some ideas seem to naturally want to be together. For these similar ideas, make up a "title" card in a different color—any idea that seems to fit can be placed in this category. Do not make these categories too broad—it is quite all right to have many different categories. Team members can have brief discussions about where the ideas should go. But do not quibble—if an idea fits into more than one category, make up a duplicate card and enter the idea in both.

Again, jot down any new ideas that come to mind (on new cards) and add them to the pool. Usually, the sorting process is accomplished rather quickly—our brain naturally likes to group and categorize ideas. Ideas that do not fit into any obvious category can be placed in the "odd ideas" category. With the title card on top, the idea cards in each category are bundled together with a rubber band. If more than seven categories are present, repeat the process by combining two or more subcategories into a new "umbrella" category. For some topics, it may be difficult to come up with category headings. In this case, sort ideas according to well-known ideas, novel ideas, and wild ideas, or according to the degree of difficulty of implementation—simple (inexpensive) ideas, complex (more challenging) ideas, and difficult ideas (requiring major resources and innovation).

TASK 2 – Developing quality ideas within a category

Each category is now worked on separately. If the team is large, categories may be assigned to heterogeneous subteams of three to five members. At the start of Task 2, conduct a brief creative thinking warm-up. The objective now is to "engineer" the many ideas or idea fragments within the category down to fewer, but more completely developed, practical, and higher-quality ideas. The team members can discuss the ideas in the category, add detail, elaborate and combine ideas. Idea synthesis—combining several concepts or ideas into a new whole - is a key mental process here.

To save time, changes and additions to ideas are made directly on the respective cards. Use paper clips to fasten cards together that have been combined into one idea, with the most developed, synthesized idea placed on top of the stack. Do not be in a hurry to discard wild ideas or ideas that do not seem to fit; try to use them as idea triggers—the most useful and innovative solution to the original problem may originate from a wild idea. Attempt to make well-known ideas better. Examine novel ideas closely but do not get carried away with one of the novel ideas—continue to look for ways to improve and synthesize all ideas in the category to come up with fewer, but higher-quality solutions. When the team has gone through all ideas in a category, the improved ideas can be written on large sheets and posted on a blackboard or wall to facilitate the next step.

TASK 3 – Force-fitting unrelated ideas between categories

The teams now try to combine the most developed ideas from all categories to come up with superior solutions. This is truly a force-fitting activity because these ideas are usually very different. Mentally try out different combinations of final ideas. Entirely new and interesting ideas and high-quality solutions may be generated through this process. Again, post the improved, final ideas. However, for some types of problems, it is impossible to distill the large number of original ideas down to a few comprehensive solutions; creative idea evaluation instead results in lists of valuable

> *You can be wrong, you can commit errors in logic, even record inconsistencies, but I won't care if you can help me to useful new combinations.*
>
> J. W. Haefele, Procter & Gamble

ideas or design criteria that, when implemented together, will solve the problem. In this case, the entire list is carried forward to idea judgment.

Then the "engineers" need to STOP! Quadrant B people may feel uncomfortable with unfinished business; they want to immediately adopt one of the final "better" ideas as the solution to the problem. Some people want to keep working to exhaustion to find a perfect solution. Others may drift into a critical mode and begin judging and tearing down the final ideas. Critical idea evaluation requires a different mindset and techniques and is the next step in the creative problem solving process.

Critical idea evaluation

Solutions to problems can be the direct causes of failures, as illustrated with a story by Galileo retold in the *American Scientist* (Nov-Dec 1992, page 525):

> *A column was stored horizontally by supporting its ends on piles of timber. But since it was possible that a column could break in the middle under its own weight (as had been observed in the past), someone suggested that a third support be added at the center. Everyone consulted agreed that this would improve the safety of the column, and the idea was implemented. A few months later, the column broke in two anyway, at the center. The cause of the failure was the new support, which failed to settle at the same rate as the end supports.*

In this step of the creative problem solving, we use critical thinking to detect and eliminate shortcomings in the proposed solutions, as well as to evaluate the risks and consequences involved, all with the purpose of finding the best solution to pass on to the "producer" to implement.

The role of "judge" in critical idea evaluation

At first glance, the judge's mindset seems to be a natural for most of us since it is easier to criticize than to explore new options or take action. However, being a "judge" can be difficult because we must determine a "best" solution from available alternatives, as represented by Figure 4.7. "Judges" need to make wise decisions based on evidence and principles, primarily using quadrant A thinking. They need a sense of timing to figure out if decisions can be made quickly or only after long, careful study, and they must also discern if the time is right for a new idea. "Judges" must detect bias and flaws (using safe-keeping quadrant B thinking) and then devise ways of overcoming the flaws with a new round of creative problem solving in quadrant C and quadrant D mode. Also, they must look ahead and consider the risks and impact of the solution. "Judges" must be

able to imagine all the things that could possibly go wrong with the solutions under consideration. This is very difficult to do for people with strong left-brain dominances. In "The Road to September 11," Newsweek, October 1, 2001, p. 41, we read, "The inability of the government to even guess that 19 suicidal terrorists might turn four jetliners into guided missiles aimed at national icons was more than a failure of intelligence. It was a failure of imagination."

Figure 4.7 *The judge's mindset*

What is good judgment?

On the warranty statement of a product, we saw this warning: "We cannot be responsible for the product used in situations which simply make no sense." With increased use of technology, good judgment becomes critically important. The precision of the computer's numerical output can give a false sense of security as to the validity of the calculations (which may have ignored factors critical to a particular situation or human interface). Good judgment also involves an awareness of bias and ethics, underlying values

> *Good judgement comes from experience. Experience comes from poor judgement.*
> Ziggy

and the presuppositions that can influence decisions. It has been said that our technological development and achievements have far outstripped moral and ethical development. Can you support this opinion with concrete evidence? Can you cite evidence supporting an opposing view?

Techniques for idea judgment

Having a list of evaluation criteria is crucial—judgment techniques work best when they are supported with a good list of criteria. We will briefly summarize some judgment techniques including the Pugh method, which is a team-based idea evaluation tool which combines the "engineer" and "judge" to develop an optimum solution.

The list of criteria

A good list of criteria includes all factors that influence a problem or decision. It takes time to make up a valid list of criteria. The list can be developed through regular brainstorming—the more criteria, the better! Through creative evaluation, the criteria are further refined, and the most useful and important criteria are selected. Make sure the evaluation is balanced between analytical and intuitive criteria, between quantitative and qualitative factors. Some people like to use a weighting system. It can simply be based on rank, for instance from 1 to 5, with the highest number assigned to the most important criteria.

Criteria can be thought of as the boundaries, limits, or specifications that the solution must fit to solve the problem. For example, applicable government laws and regulations must be observed, or the product is constrained by physical parameters. However, if time permits, limits should be questioned. Think of specifications not as chains but as challenges! Also pay attention to intuition— what attributes do you "feel" the ideal solution should have? We need to look to the future and consider factors that will make implementation easier and more successful, including people, their motivation and values, cost, support and resources, time, and consequences. Basically, criteria help us evaluate the capability of proposed ideas for solving the original problem. But rarely will an idea emerge as a clear winner that will satisfy all criteria. Thus evaluation techniques are employed to sift and rank ideas.

> *It is impossible to go through life without making judgments about people.*
> *How well you make those judgments is critical to the quality of your life.*
> *Before you judge someone else, you should judge yourself.*
> M. Scott Peck, M.D., psychiatrist and author

Quick procedures

When we do not have time to develop a good list of criteria that will allow us to rank ideas, we can use some type of *judgment by vote.* A major disadvantage of quick voting is a lack of explicit criteria since each person makes the decision based on his or her own values or prejudices. Quick votes tend to discourage the discussion of flaws. While a large number of ideas can be quickly reduced to a more manageable level through a *single criterion*, such as cost, a hasty decision here could eliminate good potential solutions.

Advantage/disadvantage techniques

The simplest approach with this type of judgment tool is to make a *separate listing of advantages and disadvantages* for each idea, with one column for all its advantages (positive marks or pros) and one column for all its disadvantages (negative marks or cons). The idea with the most advantages and least disadvantages "wins." This method has a major weakness because one negative can be so important that it could outweigh several or even all positives. When we add a third column to this evaluation to take the long-range potential of each idea into account, we have the *advantages, limitations, and potential (ALP) method.* This method makes it somewhat easier to give a fair evaluation to untried, creative ideas that depend on their potential benefits for acceptance.

If we construct an *advantage-disadvantage matrix* with the list of criteria in a column to the left and the ideas to be evaluated across the top toward the right, we have a method that compares each idea with all the others for each criterion, as illustrated in Table 14.8. Each of the five job options has advantages (+) and disadvantages (0) when evaluated against the list of brainstormed criteria. So, which option should you choose? For Job 1, the salary offer is very good, and this advantage receives a plus mark. For Job 2, the pay is low (a disadvantage) and this is scored a zero, and so on. When the matrix is completed, the scores are added separately for both marks.

In Table 14.8, Options 1 and 2 are fairly close, with the next three ranking quite a bit lower. Small differences in points are not important; thus the two top options must be considered further. Can the negatives be removed through negotiation, such as the salary offer in Job 2? When weighting factors are used, the final results may have a larger spread, and it will be easier to select the best solution. The advantage-disadvantage matrix is useful for ranking ideas and making decisions, because people working out the matrix will understand why ideas are ranked high, since they have an opportunity to discuss and modify the criteria.

Table 4.8 *Advantage/Disadvantage Matrix*

		Job Options			
List of Criteria	1	2	3	4	5
Pay	+	0	0	0	+
Other benefits	+	+	0	0	+
Personal growth	0	+	+	0	0
Good for the family	+	+	0	+	0
Independence	0	+	+	+	0
Status	0	+	0	0	+
Excitement/adventure	+	+	+	0	0
Quality co-workers	+	0	+	+	+
Supportive boss	+	+	0	+	0
Fits with life goals	+	+	0	0	+
TOTAL +	7	8	4	4	5
0	3	2	6	6	5

The QFD House of Quality is an example of a ***matrix employing weighting factors***. When the advantage-disadvantage matrix employs an existing idea or a benchmark product, process, or service as the standard against which the new concepts are compared on a three-way scale, the technique is known as ***the Pugh method***. It will be discussed in more detail in Chapter 5, since it is a very important idea evaluation and decision making tool for starting a business. As you will see, the Pugh method is an iterative technique that goes through many cycles until it results in a consensual "best" idea, concept or solution.

Other judgment techniques

When we have only a small number of ideas, the ***advocacy method*** can be used. Serious weaknesses may be overlooked, but the procedure generates excitement about innovative ideas. ***Reverse brainstorming*** is the opposite of advocacy since the weaknesses and flaws of each idea are criticized. This approach must be coupled with a strong effort of overcoming the weaknesses. When more data are required to make a judgment, ***experimentation*** may be the best tool. If only a few solutions have to be evaluated, we can choose Edison's ***trial-and-error method***. Techniques based on a statistical approach, such as the ***Taguchi method of designed experiments***, can be used for evaluating a large number of parameters and design options.

Table 4.9 *Forms of Decision Making*

Coin toss: When two options are equally good, a coin toss can help us decide quickly, since either choice will give an acceptable result.

Easy way out: When several ideas are judged equally good (including the long-term consequences), the easy way out will lead to the quickest and least painful solution.

Checklist: We can make up a checklist (list of criteria) that needs to be satisfied by the best solution. The quality of the solution will depend on the quality of the criteria.

Advantage/disadvantage matrix: We can make the decision to select the highest-ranking option (after disadvantages have been removed if possible).

Common consensus: This is the lowest level of group decision making. A decision that is reached quickly by common consensus is usually a mediocre solution because only what the majority likes and agrees with is being incorporated in the solution. When a quick decision has to be made, people tend to disregard creative ideas. Common consensus may be expedient to quickly solve an urgent problem when delay has serious consequences. For the long run, a better-quality solution should be sought.

Compromise: People with widely differing views may work out a solution through compromise—a second level of group decision making. Good parts are given up by both parties to gain acceptance of other parts. This approach is regularly used in government but may not yield the best results for the community because good features are traded off.

Compound team decision: This process—the highest level of group decision making—can result in a superior solution because the team concentrates on making the solution incorporate the best features of several ideas, to where everyone agrees that no further improvement is possible. This is the approach used in the Pugh method. In this process, what people don't like gets improved, not thrown out, to obtain a win-win outcome.

Delay or "no" decision: Delay may give you time to get more data and find a better solution, especially if circumstances have changed. Or a "no-go" decision may be the best decision. Or you may want to avoid making a decision for political reasons. By delaying the decision past a specified deadline, you can exercise the "pocket veto."

Intuitive decision: Some people make decisions intuitively, without consciously reasoning through the process or working out an explicit set of criteria. Then, to explain their decision to others, they may "invent" rational reasons for their choice. This right-brain approach works quite well with people who have learned to trust their intuition and its reliability in making good judgments in particular situations.

Decision making

The methods we have just discussed result in ranked ideas, and criteria clarify priorities—they do not make the final decision. Decision making has been defined as selecting a course of action to achieve a desired purpose. As a "judge," how can we be sure to make good decisions? We will need to appraise the situation and decide which form of decision making is most appropriate for the problem at hand. A summary of different techniques is given in Table 4.9. Important decisions with long-term effects and strong organizational impact require more thought, care and time, whereas decisions on minor issues can be made quickly and routinely. Established procedures and policies in an organization are useful since they form a framework for decision making that can reduce time and error. We must realize that it is impossible to please everyone. However, as individuals, we can make better decisions when we get into the habit of routinely using the whole-brain decision-making walk-around shown in Table 4.10. Table 4.11 is a simple and quick checklist for a "judge" that you can apply when evaluating ideas as an individual. Keep a copy in your wallet! Tables 4.10 and 4.11 are given on the following page.

Special implications of decision making for entrepreneurs

Even though strong quadrant D thinking is a primary characteristic of entrepreneurs, they also need good judgment and decision-making skills. Entrepreneurs are in charge; they are ultimately responsible for their own fortunes and often those of others, to the extent that these are under their control. This is a lonely and vulnerable position that requires a high level of self-confidence in terms of individual judgment and awareness. Self-confidence without good judgment can have disastrous consequences—it is possible to confidently make a decision that is completely wrong!

Good judgment is usually deliberate, not impulsive. For specific decisions, it can be purchased, for example by obtaining the advice of an expert consultant. Ultimately, however, the turbulence and uncertainties caused by rapidly changing economic, technological and social conditions in the twenty-first century mean that successful entrepreneurs are responsible for making decisions marginally more quickly and accurately than their competitors. Those in the process of deciding whether to start a career as an entrepreneur need to make a careful and honest assessment of their strengths and weaknesses and how these affect their ability to make rapid decisions under pressure and conditions of uncertainty. As we have seen in Chapter 2, Bhidé found that fast decision making is especially crucial when growing a business.

Table 4.10 Decision-Making Walk-Around (©1998, Ned Herrmann)

A	D
Analytical, logical, fact-based rational, bottom-line view Does my proposed decision stand up to a rational analysis of the facts? Have I considered possible bias and filters?	*Intuitive, visual, conceptual, future-oriented, big-picture view* Is my proposed decision aligned with my vision of the future? Can I live with the risks and long-range consequences?
Do the planned actions based on my proposed decision leave me with enough control? *Organized, chronological, control-oriented, detailed view* B	Are the effects on people of my proposed decision consistent with my values? *People-oriented, sensing, caring, value-based view* C

Table 4.11 Idea Judgment in a Nutshell

1. Objective	____	What is the current problem situation?
	____	What is the idea trying to do?
2. Positives	____	What is worth building on?
3. Negatives	____	What are the drawbacks?
	____	What is the worst thing that could happen?
4. Probability	____	What are the chances of success?
	____	If the idea fails, what can be learned?
5. Timing	____	Is the timing right for this idea?
	____	How long do I have to make my decision?
6. Bias	____	What assumptions am I making?
	____	Are these assumptions still valid?
	____	Do I have some blind spots?
7. The Verdict	____	What is my decision?
	____	How will it affect people?
	____	What is to be done next?

Solution implementation

The role of the "producer"

In the mindset of the producer we take action. "Producers" are managers; they have something to fight for; they are courageous, optimistic, and do not give up. They are good communicators. Implementation is time-consuming and involves several key steps. Although quadrant B planning and quadrant C

interpersonal skills are emphasized, "producers" use the entire creative problem-solving process—and the whole brain—since implementation (symbolized in Figure 4.8) is a new, very unstructured problem. Much effort, organization and attention to detail is required. Entrepreneurs as "producers" shoulder the risks involved in doing something new; they need persistence when "selling" their innovative ideas to others, for obtaining sufficient support, and for overcoming resistance.

Figure 4.8 *The producer's mindset*

The invention of the Post-it™ notes by Art Fry provides an excellent illustration of creative problem solving during implementation.

> *Post-it notes were by no means an instant success. First, Art Fry had to sell the idea to his skeptical boss who then agreed that the idea was worth testing. The two of them distributed samples throughout the company. Soon, the 3M people using them were sold on the idea. The next problem was how to produce these pads, since 3M products came in rolls only. Art Fry invented and constructed an assembly machine in the basement of his home. It took a team three years to perfect the product before 3M was ready to test-market it in four cities with eye-catching displays and large newspaper ads. The tests were an absolute failure and the company decided to kill the product.*
>
> *But Art Fry and his boss persuaded the 3M commercial office supply people to try another approach—they needed to talk to the customers. They found that people who used the product loved it and wanted more, but the others had no idea what the notes were—this product had to be experienced before it would be bought. Thus*

in the next marketing test, thousands of samples were given away. Normally, a 50-percent repurchase indicates a wild success—this test resulted in an astonishing 94-percent repurchase, and sales took off. In two years, distribution was nationwide and across Canada; the following year the product was marketed throughout Europe. Post-it notes became one of 3M's most successful office products.

The first task as "producers" is to plan your strategy. Will you have to convince others of the benefits of your idea, so they will buy and implement it, or will you and your team be in charge of the entire implementation process? You must also plan for a final evaluation of the creative problem solving process and the lessons learned.

> ### *People seldom hit what they do not aim at.*
> Henry David Thoreau
> (writer, engineer, naturalist)

Selling your idea

Gaining acceptance for your idea involves careful planning. Analyze your targeted audience; prepare a list of benefits; develop a strategy on how to make an effective sales presentation. Use the whole brain, but concentrate on quadrant C as you develop your selling strategy. The results of the Pugh method will supply much of this information.

Who is your target? Do you need to sell your idea to managers in your organization? As an inventor, do you need venture funding or help to get a patent? Determine who your audience is and what these people may want from you. Chapter 10 will provide some tips and techniques to craft an effective 30-second "sales pitch."

Why do you need a selling plan? The selling plan will prepare you to make a sale. You can have the best idea in the world, but if it is poorly presented, the result could be "no sale." You need to know some selling strategies, and you need to employ techniques that make for an effective presentation.

What are some principles of selling? Selling is not a one-shot deal—consider it in the whole context of gaining acceptance and overcoming opposition. Your success also depends on the kind of person you are—your character, your reputation, your integrity. Never jeopardize these to get a quick sale. Do not look at "making the sale'"as winning a battle of wits; think of it in terms of building long-term relationships. Learn good presentation techniques—watch your timing; be brief and to the point, use visual aids, make your ideas easy to accept by emphasizing the benefits, and avoid confrontation.

How do you deal with opposition? You can expect opposition, especially if you are working with a very creative idea! A person opposing your idea can have any number of reasons, such as lack of understanding or different priorities or loyalties to your competitors. Or they are put off because you are not "following the rules" or they fear change. Do not take opposition personally. Realize that people may take your idea as implied criticism that their way of doing something is inadequate. Dealing with opposition requires great sensitivity and diplomacy. Recruit a champion or team for extra support.

How can you make new ideas easier to accept? Demonstrate the benefits with a small pilot program or in a test market. Having a concrete prototype that can be seen and experienced with tangible results is very important. Also, if the idea doesn't work, is it possible to go back to the way things were done before, without a lot of hassle? Or can you implement the idea in easy steps requiring only small changes each time? Can you build on what is already there—in a process of continuous improvement? Does your idea fit into the culture and long-term goals of the organization?

The work plan and implementation

For preparing a work plan, the predominant thinking preference will be quadrant B, because the work plan maps out the exact steps needed for implementation—who does what, when, where, and why. You prepare time schedules and cost budgets and, as a "producer," you need to also address the prevention of possible failure. Since implementation is an unstructured problem, you must be prepared to use the other five creative problem solving mindsets to consider alternative ideas, the context, and the people interface.

The purpose of a work plan is to make sure that the idea or solution will be put to work—that it will work right and be on time as well as within budget. Different procedures are available for the work plan—some are summarized in Table 4.12. The complexity of the problem will determine which approach should be taken. Also consider the resources available to help make implementation successful.

> *In a well-organized system, all of the components work together to support each other.*
> W. Edwards Deming
> (quality expert)

Implementation monitoring and final project evaluation

After the solution has been implemented, the last remaining responsibility for "producers" is to make sure that the solution actually works. In a small project,

Table 4.12 Work Plans—Tools for Solution Implementation

Copycat: If your idea is similar to one that has been successfully implemented before, just copy the procedure, maybe with some minor adjustments, to save time and trouble.

The 5-W method: Answer the questions "who, what, where, when, and why" for each implementation task. Note that the "how" is not specified. People usually perform better when they can make their own decisions on how they will do their assigned tasks, but specify where certain critical procedures must be followed and explain why.

Flow charts: They visually present all activities that must be performed sequentially and thus are useful for showing simultaneous activities and prerequisites.

PERT (program evaluation and review technique): This method is a planning and a progress monitoring tool for large, complicated engineering projects. The chart depicts a network of interconnected activities and can identify bottlenecks and critical paths. Complex networks are handled with computer programs tracking thousands of activities. Although this detailed planning takes much effort, it leads to routine implementation.

Time/task analysis (Gantt chart): This is one of the simplest work plan formats and visually presents the time requirements of each implementation task. Every task is listed in the left-hand column of a lined chart, with the time scale across the top. For each task, a time line is drawn from starting date to the projected completion date. The chart clearly shows simultaneous or overlapping activities.

Cost budget: Information from the work plan is useful for preparing the implementation cost budget, since you will know who does what for how long. Use a standard format and work with a person who has the required accounting information.

Risk analysis: *Potential problem analysis* for risk assessment is used for very important projects where major obstacles to implementation are anticipated, but it is not cost-effective on a routine basis. Develop appropriate measures and incorporate them in your work plan for dealing with any potential risks that were identified during the critical evaluation phase.

you may be able to personally check up on the success of the implementation. Plan a first review after two weeks, followed by a second review six to twelve months later. If your project was starting a new business, plan how you will periodically track your success, not just by the bottom line but also by monitoring trends and interacting with your customers and employees. Plan to give your team positive feedback.

If you kept a journal or took notes during the entire creative problem solving process, it will be easy to write a brief summary of your results when your project has been completed. Then sit back and review what the process has done for you. What have you learned? Did it help you grow? Can you use this idea somewhere else? Did you achieve all your goals? How did the process help you communicate with people? Did the process open future opportunities for you? If the solution did not work out right, what can be learned from the experience? Keep your summary and conclusions in a file. As you complete more creative problem solving projects, this file will grow into a valuable data base.

Acitivity 4.1: Questions to think about

When the police department in Bowling Green, Ohio used an undercover narcotics agent in the disguise of a Santa Claus to nab a drug dealer, this creative (and very successful) approach caused quite an uproar in this community. Use critical quadrant A as well as contextual quadrant D thinking to answer the following questions:

1. Why do you think the creative idea ran into opposition?

   _____

   _____

2. Can you think of a recent example in your experience (at work or at home) where you have noted resistance to your own creative ideas or to the ideas of others? _____

   _____

   _____

3. From what have you learned about creative thinking and problem solving so far, who do you think needs creative problem solving skills?

   _____

   _____

An understanding of creative problem solving can help in building understanding and broader support for innovative solutions. Who needs it? Everyone!

Business development and the metaphorical mindsets

In order to gain a deeper understanding of the transition from original "brainwave" to establishing a business and market, it is helpful to consider the three distinct phases in the framework of the creative problem solving mindsets, since they identify the predominant thinking involved.

1. The creative phase

This stage refers to the emergence and development of the new concept or idea that is to be commercialized. The concept is in itself a product of creative thinking, and its assessment, evaluation, improvement and refinement also require creativity to be effective. In essence, this phase requires the "explorer" and "detective" at the outset, followed by the crucial "artist" with the assistance of the "engineer" and "judge" when the Pugh method evaluation tool is employed. This will be discussed in detail in Chapters 6, 7, and 8 in Part 2 of this book.

2. The technical phase

The progression from concept to feasibility requires appropriate technical expertise and knowledge in order to incorporate logistical requirements into the assessment and evaluation process. Thus in this phase the "engineer" predominates, assisted as needed by the "artist" and "judge." As seen in Figure 1.1 and Chapter 8, this phase occurs during the Pugh method evaluation process. This phase helps deepen our understanding of the product (or service) that constitutes the core of a new venture.

3. The market phase

With the creativity realized in terms of a technically viable concept, it is necessary to initiate a new round of creative problem solving to determine the most effective strategies for market entry and operation. All mindsets are employed, but the emphasis is on the "producer" to bring the process to a successful conclusion with sufficient attention to detailed planning and developing a customer base. Details are provided in Chapters 8, 9, and 10.

Resources for further learning

4.1 Stephen D. Brookfield, *Developing Critical Thinkers—Challenging Adults to Explore Alternative Ways of Thinking and Acting*, Jossey-Bass, San Francisco, 1988. This book shows that critical thinking is a process that helps people be more effective and innovative. Audio tapes on critical thinking by the same author and publisher are also available.

4.2 Spencer Johnson, *"Yes" or "No": The Guide to Better Decisions*, Harper Business, New York, 1992. The fictional story of a businessman's hike teaches decision-making concepts.

4.3 Charles H. Kepner and Benjamin B. Tregoe, *The Rational Manager*, McGraw-Hill, New York, 1965. This book thoroughly explains the Kepner-Tregoe method of problem solving.

4.4 Alex F. Osborn, *Applied Imagination - The Principles and Problems of Creative Problem-Solving*, 3rd rev. ed., Scribner's, New York, 1963. Recommended for team leaders.

4.5 Henry Petroski, *Design Paradigms: Case Histories of Error and Judgment in Engineering*, Cambridge University Press, New York, 1994. We can learn from other people's experience.

4.6 George M. Prince, *Practice of Creativity*, Macmillan, New York, 1970. The main topic is *Synectics*, but the book includes a discussion of the importance of the briefing document.

4.7 Arthur B. Van Gundy, Jr., *Techniques of Structured Problem Solving*, 2nd ed., Van Nostrand Reinhold, New York, 1988. Over 100 proven problem-solving methods are explained, including morphological creativity.

4.8 Roger Von Oech, *A Kick in the Seat of the Pants*, second edition, Warner Books, New York, 1998. Four roles of the creative process are presented, together with interesting stories and exercises. Optionally, the book comes with the *Creative Whack Pack*, a deck of topical cards to encourage people to think and play with ideas in new ways as they solve problems.

4.9 www.mindjet.com offers *MindManager 2002* for Palm-powered devices, and www.inspiration.com has demo versions for Windows and Macintosh. Joyce Wycoff's paperback, *Mindmapping: Your Guide to Explaining Creativity and Problem Solving*, Berkley, New York, 1991, is a paperback that expands on Tony Buzan's whole-brain technique by presenting many applications the author has taught in workshops for creative problem solving, decision making and organizational skills.

4.10 M. Neil Browne and Stuart M. Keeley, *Asking the Right Questions: A Guide to Critical Thinking* (6th edition), Prentice-Hall College Division, 2000. This popular paperback textbook is suitable for all readers from high school on up and bridges the gap from blindly accepting information to evaluating different viewpoints and making better personal decisions.

Exercises for "explorers" and "detectives"

1. **Technical Knowledge.** Predictions are that all the technological knowledge today will represent only about 1 percent of the knowledge that will be available by the Year 2050. What are the implications of this (a) for education and schools, (b) for the workplace, (c) for libraries, (d) for book publishers, (e) for authors, (f) for business, or (g) for the Internet? Brainstorm one of these topics and see if you can come up with a business idea.

2.   **The Greenhouse Effect.** Many scientists are predicting global warming. Brainstorm some positive outcomes or opportunities. For example, more air conditioners will be in demand (and will require substitutes for freon). Also, new cosmetics providing better protection from ultraviolet radiation will be needed. Come up with ten ideas on new products and markets.

3.   **Time Use Analysis.** Over the next three days, complete a detailed log on how you are using your time (in 15-minute chunks). Then do an analysis to determine which activities waste the most time. Make a Pareto diagram to find "the 20 percent that cause 80 percent of the trouble." Make a plan to eliminate the top three time wasters (one at a time).

4.   **Briefing Document Samples.** Obtain samples of briefing documents from three different organizations. How was the data collected and presented? As a team, play around with ways of improving the problem definition statement.

Exercises for "artists" and "engineers"

5.   **Warm-Up Exercise for Brainstorming Session.** Find different uses for one of the following "fun" objects: a worn sock or sneaker, a feather, a bucket of sawdust, a Frisbee, or a pumpkin.

6.   **What-if Creative Thinking Warm-Up.** Pose a what-if question and play around with it for a while, preferably in a group. The exercise is especially valuable if you do it with a wild or impossible idea.

Examples: (a) What if gravity was suspended for 10 minutes each day—how would bedrooms and bathrooms have to be redesigned? (b) What if people all looked identical—how would one be identified as an individual? (c) What if insects worldwide suddenly quadrupled in size—would this mean a new food supply or a disaster? (d) What if you were stranded on a desert island with the three people you most dislike—what would you do to make this a pleasant experience?

7.   **Disaster—So What?** Suppose that while on a vacation trip, your car with all your money and luggage is stolen. Find ten ways to turn this apparent disaster into a positive experience. Then do a creative idea evaluation—integrate these ideas into one or two practical solutions.

8.   **Sensory Experiences and Sales Ad.** First, buy a fruit or a vegetable that you have never eaten before. Note the shape, color, textures, flavor, sound-producing aspects, and fragrance—use all your senses to describe and appreciate

this new experience. Write each statement on a separate note card. Use analogies and images. Be wildly poetic! Next, sort the statements using creative idea evaluation. Combine ideas within categories and then between categories. Use one of these improved ideas and write a sales ad for this fruit or vegetable. Test your ad on several of your friends—would they want to buy?

Exercises for "judges" and "producers"

9.   **Check Your Assumptions.** Anthony and Cleopatra are found dead on the library floor in the middle of a pool of water and broken glass. Write a story of what happened. Then try to identify the hidden assumptions in your story.

10. **How to Criticize.** Make up a scenario in which you have to criticize someone. Write it in such a way that you start out with two positive statements. Then make a wishful statement about the item you want to change, followed by another positive statement about the other person. Then conclude with a hopeful, cooperative, positive statement.

11. **Authoritarian Environment.** If you live in an authoritarian environment (strict parents, teachers, boss, or political system) think about what steps you can take to be more creative and overcome the "follow the rules" mindset, yet live at peace with the authorities. Then divide into two groups of three people each, with one group representing authority, the other the creative problem solvers. Make up a scenario where a creative idea is "sold" through negotiation and compromise. Note that "breaking the rules" does not mean breaking the law. The new idea must be legal, moral, and ethical—it merely does not follow the traditional way of doing things.

12. **Evaluation of Conflicting Opinions.** Find newspaper or journal articles that give two opposing points of view on a certain subject. For example, *USA Today* carries a daily feature that presents two views on a current issue. Give a brief summary of each; then indicate your agreement or disagreement with the expressed views. Support your viewpoint with additional facts or point out where the writers should have supplied more information.

13. **Selling Technique Analyses.**
a. From the marketplace or business world, identify some selling techniques (for example, from a printed or televised **advertisement**). What makes them effective (or not effective)? What are the objectives? How well do they address customer needs? Write a brief essay.

b. Observe your **junk mail** for several weeks and collect the letters from organizations asking for support. Then analyze the content. What approaches do you find appealing and persuasive, and what approaches do you find distasteful and negative? Select the best and the worst and prepare a 2-minute presentation.

c. Analyze a recent **resume** for signs of effective selling.

Action checklist

➤   Be on the lookout for problems that you or your team can solve as you study the creative problem solving process in Part 2 of the book. The hands-on application is crucial to enhance your learning by providing tacit, experiential knowledge.

➤   To practice the mindset of an explorer, take one afternoon a month to look around in a subject you don't know anything about, by reading, speaking to people, visiting exhibits, or attending a lecture. Block off this time right now in your calendar.

➤   Once a month, alone or with others, brainstorm answers to the paradigm shift question (Ref. 1.3): "What is impossible to do in my field or organization today, but if it could be done, would fundamentally change what I do?" Jot down the ideas in a notebook.

➤   Think about applications for brainstorming in your daily life. For fun, schedule a brainstorming session at a party to create a song, dance, or children's storybook.

➤   When you are tempted to criticize someone's idea, try to use the imperfect idea as a stepping-stone and generate at least three "better" ideas. Or come up with your own idea and then work with the other person to integrate both ideas into one solution.

➤   Analyze a case in the past where you made what you feel was a "wrong" decision. What aspect of the judgment process should you improve to prevent this from happening again?

➤   Take the time to learn how to do mind mapping (if you are not familiar with this right-brain thinking tool).

Chapter 5
The Pugh Method

First, an overview of the Pugh method of creative concept evaluation is presented. Although this evaluation method had its origins in engineering design, it can be used to evaluate many different types of concepts, alternatives, proposals, bids, options, choices, and ideas, as will be illustrated with a detailed case study. Another detailed "teaching" example can be accessed from a website.

Overview of the Pugh method
Why was the Pugh method developed?

The Pugh method of creative design concept evaluation was developed by Stuart Pugh, a design and project engineer with many years of practice in industry. He later became professor and head of the design division at the University of Strathclyde in Scotland. He came to recognize that designs done purely by analysis were "somewhat less than adequate" because it took a long cycle of modifications to satisfy the customer. He realized that engineers need to see the whole picture in product design and development; they need an integrated approach to be competitive. Although the Pugh method has its most direct application in product design, the procedure and thinking skills used can be applied to many other situations where different ideas and options have to be evaluated to find an optimum solution. For example, as you will see in Part 2, the outcome of the Pugh method in evaluating business concepts will feed directly into the business plan.

What is the Pugh method?

It is a creative concept evaluation technique that uses criteria (usually derived from "the voice of the customer") in an advantage-disadvantage matrix. The best existing concept (which in a business enterprise can be a product, process or service) is used as datum against which the new concepts are compared. In the process of completing the evaluation matrix, new ideas are generated and thus new and improved concepts are added to the matrix. This process is repeated several times until a superior concept emerges which will have all negatives (flaws) removed. Because the concepts are evaluated side-by-side in the matrix, the process encourages force-fitting and synthesis on the conscious and subconscious level. The exploration of many different alternatives on how to satisfy the criteria is encouraged before beginning the evaluation process.

What are the benefits of the Pugh method?

1. All participants (an individual, a small team, or several different teams) gain insight into the problem and a clear understanding of the criteria which are becoming increasingly better defined.

2. The Pugh method is an effective communications tool.

3. All customers (manufacturing, sales, service, the impact on individuals and society) are considered, not just the purchaser or end user of the concept.

4. When teams are involved, the discussion can lead to creative leaps between different concepts and subsequent idea synthesis, as flaws are attacked together and the teams experience synergy.

5. The resulting new concepts are better than the original ideas. No flaws are overlooked; invulnerable products or services are developed that will succeed in a competitive market.

6. The participants develop consensus about the best solution; they understand its strength and champion the concept.

7. It prevents a business from making costly mistakes in the choice of products and leads to many other cost savings and applications.

8. In the case of complete concepts (such as submitted proposals or bids), the Pugh method is used for a single round to identify the best among the competing proposals. In addition, the evaluation will identify areas of weakness, thus making it possible to ask proposers to make modifications before receiving funding or go-ahead.

What are the steps in the Pugh method?

The Pugh method has two phases, where each phase differs in emphasis. In Phase 1, the focus is on generating creative concepts in several rounds of increasing quality. In Phase 2, the iterative process converges to an optimum solution.

PHASE 1 STEPS

1. The list of evaluation criteria is developed and the datum (benchmark) is selected, usually the best existing product. When no suitable existing product exists, one of the new concepts is chosen at random to be the datum.

2. Original concepts are brainstormed, and conceptual sketches or descriptions are prepared.

3. Each concept is discussed and evaluated against the datum. New concepts that emerge are added to the matrix. When an individual uses the method, the process must still be written down and the thinking and decisions documented.

4. The first-round results are evaluated; the top-ranked concept becomes the new datum, and the designs or concepts are improved for the next round and then evaluated.

5. This evaluation and improvement process is continued for one or more additional rounds, each time using the highest-scoring concept as the new datum—depending on the complexity of the problem and the time available.

PHASE 2 STEPS

6. Weaker concepts are now dropped. The evaluation is continued with increasingly stronger concepts (which are "engineered" or developed to more detail). Criteria are expanded and refined. The participants continue to gain valuable insight into the problem and proposed solutions.

7. The process converges to a strong consensus solution that cannot be improved further. The team or individual is committed to this superior concept.

Is there a "fast-track" version for simple problems?

Phase 1 is conducted using Steps 1-4 above. Then the highest scoring concept of Round 2 is closely examined. If possible, any identified weaknesses are eliminated with features from the other concepts or additional creative ideas—this then becomes the final concept.

What are "concepts"?

Concepts can be ideas or any type of solution to a defined problem, not just engineering designs. Concepts in this context meet a list of criteria, customer needs, or design specifications. According to Professor Pugh, concepts are often best generated by individuals, but concept selection, synthesis, and optimization are often best performed in groups. "Generate as many ideas as possible—single solutions are usually a disaster" (Ref. 5.1, pages 69, 71).

Concepts are usually worked out in sufficient detail to allow a rough estimate of cost and feasibility and a determination of major features. A description or preferably a sketch of each concept is prepared on a large sheet of paper (that will be visible to everyone in the room when posted on a wall above the evaluation matrix) whenever a team is involved in the evaluation. The communication of the concept (description and sketch) must be such that others clearly understand it.

How does the evalution matrix work?

It is highly recommended that a heterogeneous team be used for conducting the Pugh evaluation. The evaluation meeting is held in an ample conference room with a large board covering an entire wall. An evaluation matrix is set up on the board, with the evaluation criteria listed in the left-hand column of the matrix. The large sketches or brief descriptions of the concepts are posted across the top of the matrix, with the datum posted first. The

Pugh Method Evaluation Scale	
+	means substantially better
–	means clearly worse
S	means more or less the same

main features of each concept (including the datum) are explained by its champions. Right after each presentation, the concept is evaluated against the datum, using the three-way rating scale given in the box. The three-way evaluation may appear rather primitive, but it is easy to do with a team. The results are effective, because the objective is not quantitative, precise information but a movement toward increasing quality and superior satisfaction of all criteria. Inexperienced teams may be very defensive of their concept and will argue about every minus mark. They need to remember that this evaluation serves to point out weaknesses or potential problems in the concept that must be overcome for it to be viable (and for the survival of the business). The judgment only determines as objectively as possible if the concept is better or worse than the datum or benchmark for each criterion.

What if an individual does the evaluation?

When we are the sole evaluator of our own ideas, we must be careful to analyze possible bias and blind spots. We also must guard against falling in love with a particular concept before generating and developing several viable alternatives. All concepts must be evaluated fairly and critically.

What do you do with the first-round results?

The first-round matrix is critically examined. Is there a criterion that received no plus signs all across the matrix? This indicates that none of the new concepts addressed an important customer need or solution requirement—a critical omission. If a criterion received all positives, it will need to be refined and made more specific. Criteria that are least important can be dropped in future rounds; new criteria that clarify an ambiguity are added. Typically, the customers become more precisely identified. The scores in each column are added separately for the positives and the negatives. The ultimate goal of the process is to obtain concepts whose shortcomings have all been eliminated creatively. The concepts are taken back to the "drawing board" and improvements are targeted to the identified weaknesses in preparation for the next round of evaluation. The concept with the highest number of positives is chosen as the new datum. Its creators will try to improve this design by borrowing good ideas from other concepts to address weaknesses. The improved concepts now have to beat a higher standard to remain in the running. Phase 1 evaluations are continued for at least one more round for relatively simple concepts— complicated designs and solutions may require two or three additional rounds.

What happens in Phase 2?

Here, the emphasis changes from conceiving additional creative concepts to synthesizing higher-quality solutions by combining ideas and dropping the weaker concepts. During the process, the strong, surviving concepts are "engineered" or developed to more detail; the criteria are expanded and further refined. Cost, market, feasibility and engineering analyses are conducted as applicable. The process converges to a strong consensus concept that cannot be overturned by a better idea—all good points have been defended and all negatives eliminated. Everyone is committed to this concept which is now ready for prototyping to demonstrate the concept and for developing into a commercial product.

What if a negative cannot be eliminated?

Costs that are higher than the datum are often a negative criterion that cannot be eliminated. If a competitive price is very important, other concepts that do not have this "flaw" will have to be pursued. This could be an area where new technology may be deployed. For a manufactured product, Taguchi methods can be used to reduce cost while increasing quality. Alternatively, innovative marketing may have to be invented to convince the customers that the value added by the new product is worth the increased price. Examples are the Post-it notes or the Federal Express package delivery system. It must be remembered that the Pugh method does not make the final decisions—it is a judgment tool, and the responsibility for making the final decision rests with the individual or team using the tool. If the problem is very complex, additional resources must be employed (experts or analytical tools such as QFD or FMEA).

Examples

Simple example—design of an improved lamp

A class of high school honor students in an engineering summer program found inconvenient lamp switches to be a problem which needed to be addressed with new lamp designs. They conducted a customer survey, did a Pareto analysis, brainstormed ideas for solving the identified problems, and developed a list of design criteria. Teams came up with three different types of design concepts: improvements over existing table lamps; innovative—completely new—concepts, and novelty lamps. The novelty lamps did not score well in the first-round evaluation. For the second round, a traditional lamp with many improvements (built-in timer switch in the base, flexible shade, retractable cord, and fluorescent bulb) was the datum. An innovative design scored very high in this round. It could be used as a table or a pole lamp, and its shade could be fixed for up-down indirect or task lighting or expanded to expose a lighted column for room lighting. The novelty lamp received mostly negative marks, yet the team remained steadfast in not wanting to change its concept; it had "fallen in love" with its design—a fatal flaw in product design which was identified with the Pugh method. Lack of time and resources prevented the high-scoring team from pursuing its invention which had the potential to be patented and generated much audience interest.

Teaching example – car horn design

A detailed "teaching" example for the design of a car horn has been developed by Professor Pugh. We have adapted and simplified it to bring out different points in the *Teaching Manual for Creative Problem Solving and Engineering Design*. The example with discussion can be found at **www.engineering-creativity.com** in File 8, pages 17-20.

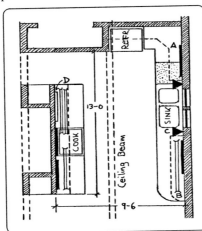

Figure 5.1 *Kitchen Layout*

Current example – dark kitchen needs improved lighting

Problem Briefing: A large kitchen in a house built in the late 1940s is quite dark at night, especially at the sink and the chopping board to the left, although large windows admit ample daylight. The slightly sloped cherry-paneled ceiling has an average height of 10 ft 9 in. and is traversed by a 14 x 6-in. wood-laminate beam supporting the flat roof immediately above, as indicated in Figure 5.1. The walls are painted beige; the cabinets are metal—beige above the counter, brick red below. The countertop is beige, and the vinyl floor has a brownish brick pattern. Table 5.1 lists the existing lighting fixtures. The fluorescent tubes lying on top of the cabinets are plugged into outlets above the cabinets (all on the same circuit) and switched on/off at the kitchen entrances. All other fixtures are on individual switches. The spotlights over the sink are ugly and do not keep their aimed direction well. The chrome triangular under-cabinet fixtures are quaint but have a rather dim light output. All five plugged-in fluorescent tubes look cheap and are hard to clean; the 2-ft tube is rarely if ever used.

Table 5.1 *Existing Kitchen Lighting Fixtures*

I.D.	#, Rating	Type Fixture	Location
A	4, 20 Watt	2-ft fluorescent triangular	under wall cabinets
B	4, 40 Watt	4-ft fluorescent tubes	on top of cabinets
C	2, 75 Watt	Incandescent spot in can	5-ft above sink
D	1, 20 Watt	2-ft fluorescent tube	under microwave

Problem Definition Statement: Improve the general and task lighting in the kitchen shown in Figure 5.1 while upgrading the lamp quality and matching or complementing the style of the lighting fixtures in the adjacent dining and living rooms, at reasonable cost and without remodeling the kitchen or covering up the beauty of the existing paneled ceiling.

Round 1 Concepts, Performance Criteria and Evaluation: The concepts for improving the lighting in this kitchen are listed in Table 5.2. The criteria are listed in the Round 1 Pugh evaluation matrix shown in Table 5.3. The current lighting is taken as the datum. None of the options provide a standout solution for solving the problem. However, the evaluation makes it clear that a second meeting with the lighting supplier is necessary to explore further options and get more information. Also, some of the criteria will need to be expanded and made more specific.

Round 2 Concepts and Evaluation: Option #5—the halogen fixture—becomes the new datum for Round 2 since it had the highest number of positives. The aim for Round 2 is to try and combine concepts to eliminate negatives and supply more detail. These concepts are listed in Table 5.4. The painting option is put off to a future time because of little return for the costs involved. The Round 2 matrix is shown in Table 5.5. Note that in Table 5.5, S is also used to indicate neutral or not applicable.

Table 5.2 *Options for Round 1 of the Pugh Evaluation Matrix*

---

1. **Track Lighting** – Install an 8-ft long track with 4 movable spots (250 Watt each, black), to match existing track light in adjacent living room. Plug into outlet over cabinet near sink.

2. **Sink Task Lighting** – Replace the two spotlights over the sink with new, nicer-looking, and more efficient, practical lamps.

3. **Over-Cabinet Strip Lighting** – Replace the fluorescent tubes with a lighted strip along the top of all wall cabinets.

4. **Fluorescent Hanging Fixtures** – Install two 4-ft fluorescent fixtures with efficient diffusers at 8-ft level. Hang with chains from ceiling (not from the off-center beam), with wood wurrounds, to replace the over-the-cabinet tubes; wire to main switch. Option explored with supplier.

5. **Halogen Fixtures** – Install two hanging halogen down lights; wire to main switch; match chrome style of under-cabinet triangular fixtures. Option explored with supplier.

6. **Brighter Surfaces** – Paint walls white; install white vinyl flooring; install new white countertop; paint cherry panels in ceiling white.

Table 5.3 *Round 1 Kitchen Lighting Concept Evaluation*

Criteria Concepts:	Now	1	2	3	4	5	6
1. Adequate sink task light		S	+	-	+	+	-
2. Other countertop lighting		-	S	-	+	+	-
3. General lighting	D	S	S	S	+	+	+
4. Light to ceiling	A	-	S	+	-	-	+
5. Energy efficient	T	-	+	-	+	+	+
6. Easy to clean	U	+	S	S	S	+	-
7. Easy bulb replacement	M	+	S	-	S	+	S
8. Allow deletion of tubes		-	-	+	-	-	-
9. Matching room styles		+	+	-	-	-	S
10. Attractive high-tech look		+	+	+	+	+	S
11. Low labor cost		-	+	+	-	-	-
12. Low materials cost		-	-	-	-	-	-
TOTAL POSITIVES (+)		4	5	4	5	7	3
TOTAL NEGATIVES (-)		6	2	6	5	5	6

Table 5.4 *Options for Round 2 of the Pugh Evaluation Matrix*

7. Fluorescent Track Lighting – Install a black 8-ft long, 2-circuit track with 3 movable cans (150 Watt incandescent bulbs or fluorescent bulb option) and one 2-ft fluorescent, 40 Watt movable parabolic louvered diffuser ("wall washer") to match existing track light in adjacent living room. Mount to bottom of beam; connect to main switches with conduit along beam/ceiling edge.

8. Sink Task Lighting – Replace the two spotlights over the sink with black cans matching the track light of Option #1. Use fluorescent bulbs.

9. Over-Cabinet Strip Lighting – Replace the fluorescent tubes with a rope light along the top of all wall cabinets.

10. Fluorescent Hanging Fixtures – Install two 4-ft fluorescent fixtures with efficient diffusers at 8-ft level (sleek high-tech design); hang from ceiling; centered between counters.

11. Halogen Fixtures – Install two hanging halogen down lights; wire to main switch; match style of dining room chandelier if possible.

Table 5.5 *Round 2 Kitchen Lighting Concept Evaluation*

Criteria Concepts:	5	7	8	9	10	11
1. Adequate sink task light		S	+	-	S	S
2. Countertop lighting (window wall)		+	+	-	S	S
3. Countertop lighting (cooktop wall)	D	-	-	-	S	S
4. Light to ceiling	A	S	S	+	S	S
5. Low-energy night lighting	T	S	+	+	S	S
6. Low glare	U	+	+	+	+	S
7. Flexible (direction, additions, lumens)	M	+	+	-	S	S
8. Easy bulb replacement		S	S	-	-	S
9. Energy efficient		S	S	-	S	S
10. Easy to clean		S	S	-	S	S
11. Preserves view of ceiling/open space		S	+	+	-	S
12. Allow deletion of tubes		+	-	+	S	S
13. Matching room styles		+	+	S	-	+
14. Attractive to future owners		+	+	-	-	S
15. Low labor cost		S	+	+	S	S
16. Low materials cost		-	+	-	+	S
TOTAL POSITIVES (+)		6	10	6	2	1
TOTAL NEGATIVES (-)		2	2	9	4	0

Since Concept #11 has no negatives, does this mean that it is the optimum solution? Not necessarily—as you will see, it will rank very differently when evaluated against the new datum. The over-the-counter strip-lighting option is now eliminated as not being cost effective. And the fluorescent hanging fixture is eliminated because it is too intrusive.

Round 3 Concepts and Evaluation: Concept #8 had the highest number of positives and is thus the datum for Round 3. Concepts #7 and #8 are combined as Concept #12 (see Table 5.6). This allows for even lighting of both kitchen sidewalls with an additional "wall washer." Concept #11 is carried forward unchanged. The Round 3 matrix is shown in Table 5.7.

Table 5.6 *Options for Round 3 of the Pugh Evaluation Matrix*

> **11. Two Halogen Fixtures** – Install two hanging halogen down lights; wire to main switch. Match the style of the glass shades with the style of the dining room chandelier if possible.
>
> **12. Fluorescent Track Lighting System** – Install a black 8-ft long, 2-circuit track with two movable cans with fluorescent bulbs and two 2-ft fluorescent, 40 Watt movable parabolic louvered diffusers. Mount to bottom of beam; connect to main switches with conduit along beam/ceiling edge. Replace the two spotlights over the sink with matching cans and fluorescent bulbs to achieve a flexible, attractive, and easily modified, adjustable lighting system.

"Best" Solution and Concluding Comments on Process: The concept that ultimately was incorporated into the "best" solution was generated for Round 2 by combining the track lighting and fluorescent bulb concept. The supplier suggested this option, and the owner was able to see a similar installation in a store nearby. Combining the track lighting and the over-the-sink fixture into a matching system optimized the solution, and the merits of this solution are confirmed by the Round 3 evaluation. This solution satisfies the original problem. A very strong "selling point" is the built-in flexibility which easily allows future modification if necessary or desired. It also allows for on-site adjustments after installation, again depending on changing needs. With this solution, the over-the-counter 4-ft fluorescent tubes were eliminated, since the 2-ft fluorescent "wall washers" provide very bright but diffused light. The total cost of $742 was acceptable, since the system is highly functional as well as attractive. The Pugh method was crucial for clarifying criteria, for generating viable options and for identifying the optimal solution. The homeowners are very pleased with the new lighting system.

Table 5.7 *Round 3 Kitchen Lighting Concept Evaluation*

Criteria Concepts:	8	11	12
1. Adequate sink task light		-	+
2. Countertop lighting (along window wall)		-	+
3. Countertop lighting (along cooktop wall)		-	+
4. Indirect light to ceiling (eliminate "cave" look)	D	S	+
5. Low-energy night lighting	A	-	+
6. Low glare, especially for eyeglass wearers	T	-	+
7. Flexibility in direction, light level, future additions	U	-	+
8. Easy bulb replacement (with step stool, not ladder)	M	S	S
9. Energy efficient, cool burning		-	S
10. Sun-type light quality		+	+
11. Easy to clean of kitchen grease buildup		S	S
12. Preserves view of beautiful paneled ceiling		-	S
13. Allows deletion of all existing plugged-in tubes		-	+
14. Matching adjoining dining and living room fixtures		S	S
15. Attractive to future owners; good "selling point"		-	+
16. Reasonable installation costs		S	S
17. Material cost in line with "value added"		S	S
TOTAL POSITIVES (+)		1	10
TOTAL NEGATIVES (-)		10	0

Note: An individual, not a team, conducted this application of the Pugh method for evaluating different options and developing a "best" solution. It illustrates that this evaluation technique can be used profitably by anyone, as long as the evaluator maintains an unbiased viewpoint when judging each concept and obtains information and ideas from experts as needed for ,developing good alternatives, as shown in this example.

Resources for further learning

Reference

5.1 Stuart Pugh, *Total Design: Integrated Methods for Successful Product Engineering*, Addison-Wesley, New York, 1991. This book provides the framework of a disciplined design and evaluation method for creating products that satisfy the needs of the customer. It includes examples from many fields and a wide selection of design exercises.

Exercises

1.   **Application to a Current Problem or Project.** Along the lines of the kitchen lighting exercise, select a project in your life—either alone or with a small team of friends, colleagues or family members—where you have (or need to develop) several options. Use the Pugh method to find and "engineer" an optimum solution; then summarize what you have learned about this creative idea evaluation tool.

2.   **Redesign of Hourglass Timer**. Design a simple hourglass timer that makes a sound when time is up—a useful feature for avoiding arguments in the heat of a game or competition. Come up with at least three different concepts —then evaluate them with the Pugh "fast-track" approach.

3.   **Improve a Business Procedure.** Think of a business process, paperwork, or way of doing something that could be simplified or made more efficient through creative thinking. Brainstorm a list of criteria and develop alternate solutions; then find the "best" using the Pugh evaluation in two or more rounds.

Action checklist

➤   Take the time to get into the web site to look at the evaluation matrix (page 20) of the car horn example and read the associated discussion.

➤   Teach the Pugh method to someone else by going through an actual application at home or on the job.

➤   If you are planning to start a business, you will have many opportunities to use the Pugh method, beginning with the selection of your product, market niche, and so on. Now, you can immediately continue into Part 2 of this book for additional information, illustrations, and resources geared to enterprise development and startup. Then have fun with the implementation!

➤   Think about what you have learned from Part 1 of this book. In your notebook, write down some ideas of how you can apply what you have learned in your life and on the job. Then look at Figures 6.1, 7.1, 8.1, 9.1 and 10.1 in Part 2 and survey the content of the respective chapters and how the various topics are arranged to reinforce the different thinking skills and problem-solving mindsets. Practice these skills in many different situations, and use the book as a resource to further hone your skills and expand the range of possible applications.

PART 2

Application:
How to Be a Creative
Entrepreneur

"HAZARD WARNING"

At this point in our book we feel it is important to issue a "hazard warning" before proceeding further. With the information and observations presented in Part 1 of this book you will be better equipped to generate creative ideas and to solve problems more effectively–should you choose to apply the methods described. As indicated earlier, these techniques can be applied in many and various situations to make life more interesting and productive.

Part 2 of this book will extend your understanding and grasp of the importance of what you have learned so far by embedding it in the entrepreneurial process itself. If you choose to follow this route, then do so in full recognition of the following "hazard warnings":

* Most new business ideas never reach the market.

* The person who is likely to be exploited in terms of unreasonable working hours, poorly specified responsibilities, low pay, anxiety, and stress **will be you!**

* Parts 1 and 2 of this book will help you reduce the probability of failure, but the only advice that will reduce that chance to zero is given by someone who says, "Stop; don't be entrepreneurial; don't even think about it; play it safe!"

* We can make one promise—learning to think more creatively and entrepreneurially will change your life.

* Finally, it is worth observing that genuine entrepreneurs, whether they be successful or not, would take absolutely no notice whatsoever of the warnings set out above.

Chapter 6
Finding a Problem to Solve

Now that you have worked through Part 1 of this book, are you determined to start your own business enterprise or at least explore the idea? Or are you looking for some additional illustrations of how the creative problem solving process can be applied? In either case, Part 2 of this book will offer a plethora of ideas to think about as well as practical information for actually carrying out the development of a creative entrepreneurial idea "from brain to market."

In this chapter, we want to first explore areas where you might find a business idea. We will provide "explorer" and "detective" tools to help you identify potential problem areas and will present the special requirements for documenting an invention. Because the market—your customers—ultimately determines the success of your venture, we will offer some tips on how to identify the "real" problem (and the "real" customers). As illustrated in Figure 6.1, we use both divergent and convergent thinking modes as we identify, focus and define a customer need or problem to solve.

Individual and societal problems

Economic development at its best is often referred to as "Pareto optimal"—it increases economic welfare without causing a reduction in the welfare of any other individual or groups. This principle is central to the application of the creative problem solving process. Individual and societal problems often constrain economic development. Conversely, new ventures create opportunities—people are free to pursue their dream to their own benefit, but in the process they create new jobs for others and possibly also new industries, leading to economic development and social mobility. Therefore, problems represent potential areas for applying new ideas and enterprises and may range from the minor inconveniences associated with everyday life to the major challenges of our times confronting society.

> *Breakthrough ideas are most likely to occur when you are actively, confidently searching for new opportunities.*
> Denis Waitley and Robert Tucker

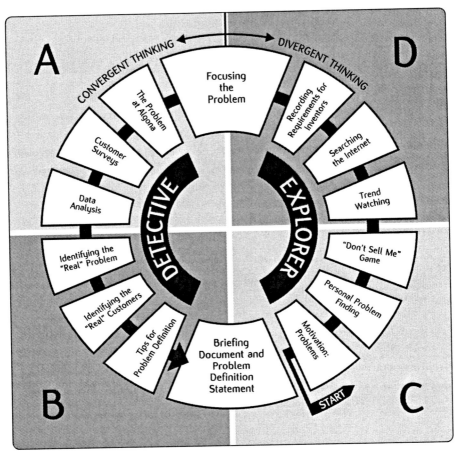

Figure 6.1 Thinking tasks and just-in-time learning for finding a customer need or problem to solve (superimposed on the four-quadrant ABCD model developed by Ned Herrmann)

Potential sources of new ideas and approaches can be found by considering aspects of our lives and experiences that could be significantly improved by the appropriate economic development. It is often assumed that entrepreneurs are prompted into action by the belief that they have a particularly appropriate and possibly unique solution to a prevailing problem for which people would be prepared to pay good money. This responsive alertness to opportunities is a characteristic of the Austrian school's view of entrepreneurs as described in Chapter 2. We believe that this interpretation can be taken a step further by encouraging the potential entrepreneur to actively seek out opportunities by adopting an explorer's mindset to discover new areas of activity that have not been addressed before.

Using the explorer's mindset

In Chapter 4, we presented an overview of different tools that can be used to identify an opportunity or clarify a problem area. Here, we will give some additional tips and guidelines to help you toward finding a problem area with a good potential for generating a viable enterprise.

Personal problem finding

Listing problems is a first step to help you decide which ones may be worth solving. It transforms a body of information into a set of components that can then be restructured, redefined, checked, and searched. Keep a journal of problems that you find personally interesting and that might be worth your while to resolve. You may chance upon a problem area with a large potential market for a good solution. The personal questions in Table 6.1 and the list of business challenges in Table 6.2 may help you get started.

Table 6.1 *Personal List of Questions*

1. What would you like to have or to accomplish?
2. What would you like to do better?
3. What do you wish would happen in your job (or study area)?
4. What do you wish you had more time to do?
5. What are your unfulfilled goals?
6. What more would you like to get out of your job?
7. What excites you in your work (and in your hobbies)?
8. What annoys you in your environment or angers you at work?
9. What have you (or others) recently complained about?
10. What would you like to get others to do?
11. What changes would you like to introduce?
12. What takes too long? What is wasted? What is too complicated?
13. In what ways are you inefficient?
14. Where are the bottlenecks? What wears you out?
15. What in your job turns you off?
16. In what ways could you make more money?
17. What misunderstandings have you encountered recently?

Let some of the questions in Tables 6.1 and 6.2 incubate in your mind for a while. The following game has a double purpose—it can warm up your right-brain thinking modes while at the same time give you insight into a technique that can help you identify customer needs and viewpoints. So let's have some fun in the explorer's mindset!

Table 6.2 *Typical Business Challenges*

1.	What business idea would you like to work on?
2.	What business relationship would you like to improve?
3.	What new product is needed to satisfy a customer want?
4.	How can you cut costs and increase production?
5.	How can you better differentiate an existing product from all the others?
6.	What extension of a current product's market is needed?
7.	How can you sell 20 percent more than you are at present?
8.	How can you become indispensable to your company?
9.	How can customer complaints be handled better?
10.	How can you improve the role service plays in the sale of your products?
11.	How can you become more customer-oriented?
12.	In what ways might you outperform the competition?
13.	Which of your products can you make into a true innovation and market leader?
14.	What is an important issue or challenge for you in your present business?

The "Don't sell me" game

Objectives:

The game is based on what people want and respond to in order to have their basic needs and desires satisfied. For example:

Don't sell me clothes;   ...   sell me attractiveness.
Don't sell me shoes;   ...   sell me feet that feel refreshed and energized.
Don't sell me books;   ...   sell me knowledge that makes me successful.
Don't sell me the Beatles;   ...   sell me a nostalgic mood and great memories.

The game forces you to zero in on intangibles and use words to communicate different ideas. It asks you to think more about implications, less about the task itself. It moves your perspective away from things and more toward feelings, hopes, emotions, and benefits. "Don't sell me" is the scenic route to new awareness of the essence of your task. It takes you right to your mission's core, but from a variety of emotional directions. An individual or team that is low in quadrant C thinking preference may find this very difficult to do at first, but don't give up too soon!

Instructions:

1. Define your mission. What are you trying to accomplish or change? Who is your audience? Using the work sheet on the next page, complete the following statement:

   Don't sell me _____ *(your task in concrete terms)*.

   Sell me _____ *(your task in abstract term)*.

   Complete each statement as quickly as you can. Fill in the blank a dozen times or more. Let your pen move. You're looking for "soft" stuff—the feelings, emotions, attitudes, results, consequences, secondary benefits, gut instincts, intuitions, and perceptions that drive your day-to-day existence.

2. After completing the statements, set the list aside for ten minutes and do something else. Let it incubate; let your subconscious do some of the work.

3. When you return to your list, focus on each completed statement, one at a time. Concentrate on the pieces, not the aggregate, since you can quickly become overwhelmed when you attack a problem in its totality. Do some divergent thinking now. Use each one of your statements as a springboard to new ideas. What new thoughts does each statement prompt? Look at each statement as an opportunity to solve a part of the task. Consider each as an element of the challenge, or a new direction from which to approach the challenge. Let each represent a separate need. Address emotions, feelings, and perceptions. Look for weaknesses to fix and strengths to trumpet. If you have worked alone or with one partner up to this point, make up a group of three or four members to add diversity to your thinking.

Practice problem:

If you are having difficulties playing the game in a pre-selected problem area, practice first with one of these three topics:

Don't sell me CREATIVITY BOOKS ...

        Sell me _____

Don't sell me SOFT DRINKS ...

        Sell me _____

Don't sell me a FINANCIAL PLAN ...

        Sell me _____

Work Sheet

Sell me _____

Sell me _____

Sell me _____

Sell me _____

Sell me _____

Sell me _____

Sell me _____

Sell me _____

Sell me _____

Sell me _____

Sell me _____

Sell me _____

Sell me _____

Sell me _____

Sell me _____

Sell me _____

Sell me _____

Sell me _____

Sell me _____

Sell me _____

Sell me _____

Sell me _____

Sell me _____

Sell me _____

Sell me _____

Some answers to get you going:

Don't sell me CREATIVITY BOOKS ...
> Sell me "confidence in my brain."

Don't sell me CREATIVITY BOOKS ...
> Sell me "creative juice."

Don't sell me CREATIVITY BOOKS ...
> Sell me "a renewal of my childhood."

Don't sell me CREATIVITY BOOKS ...
> Sell me "success in the corporate world."

Don't sell me CREATIVITY BOOKS ...
> Sell me "a life I can be excited about."

Don't sell me CREATIVITY BOOKS ...
> Sell me "a blueprint for greatness."

Don't sell me CREATIVITY BOOKS ...
> Sell me "lasting enthusiasm and energy."

Don't sell me CREATIVITY BOOKS ...
> Sell me "a way to discover my real self."

Don't sell me CREATIVITY BOOKS ...
> Sell me "a leadership tool."

The idea of "confidence in my brain" or "lasting enthusiasm and energy" help us think about the importance of courage and a positive outlook, along with the inspiration and wherewithal to challenge conformity. The ideas of "success in the corporate world" and "a life I can be excited about" underline the importance of examples of creativity techniques in action, in both professional and personal contexts.

Don't sell me SOFT DRINKS ... Sell me "good taste and flavor."
Don't sell me SOFT DRINKS ... Sell me "outrageousness."
Don't sell me SOFT DRINKS ... Sell me "refreshment."
Don't sell me SOFT DRINKS ... Sell me "a fun break in the day."
Don't sell me SOFT DRINKS ... Sell me "excitement and adventure."
Don't sell me SOFT DRINKS ... Sell me "revolution."
Don't sell me SOFT DRINKS ... Sell me "perpetual youth."
Don't sell me SOFT DRINKS ... Sell me "freedom."
Don't sell me SOFT DRINKS ... Sell me "a piece of the tropics."

While soft drinks are about flavor, taste, refreshment, and slaking thirst, they are more than that. They are part of our lives, a reflection of our culture, and a symbol of youth.

Activity 6.1: Developing "sell me" statements for a financial plan.

Don't sell me a FINANCIAL PLAN ...

Sell me

_____

_____

_____

_____

_____

_____

_____

_____

_____

_____

Trend watching

As we have seen earlier (refer to Table 4.3 for tips), one of the most important "explorer" tools is watching for trends. When you scan the messages bombarding you daily through news and advertisements in the media, be constantly on the lookout for developing trends. Use a variety of sources: TV, newspapers, radio talk shows, professional journals and magazines. Some trends can be expected to last a long time (for example, those involving demographics and census data). An example is that the population in the Western cultures is getting older. Thus we have the problem of the "sandwich" generation: middle-aged parents being squeezed by responsibilities in caring for elderly parents while assisting their own children with careers or helping to care for grandchildren. In other cultures, the majority of the population is young—under 25 years old (which creates very different problems and opportunities, for example in the area of basic and high-tech education).

The longevity of some trends is difficult to predict. How long will the demand for increased security, especially for the traveling public, persist, when the threat of imminent terrorist attacks has abated? Ideas that will help airlines reduce the long lines and waiting times at security checkpoints while maintaining security would certainly be welcomed with open arms. Timing is important. In the mid-1970s, energy conservation became a key issue, with oil prices skyrocketing and periodic shortages. In early 2002, energy prices are at a very low point—but the question is for how long, since oil supplies are vulnerable to the volatile political conditions in the Middle East and Venezuela?

Searching the Internet

The world wide web is a wonderful explorer tool in several ways. It has many web sites on creative thinking. You can get business ideas and ideas for inventions from specific sites, or you can surf the web to get more information on problems and their context. Patent searching in patent depository libraries used to be very time-consuming and tedious—now you can do preliminary patent searches right from your desktop. Some relevant starting sites for all these tasks are listed in Table 6.3.

Table 6.3 *Useful Web Sites*

Creativity	
www.cul.co.uk	Book reviews and creativity software (some free).
www.AmCreativityAssoc.org	Check out the "creativity igniter" articles.
www.edwdebono.com	Lateral thinking; weekly message; games.
Preliminary Patent Search and Information for Inventors	
www.inventnet.com	Patent searching tutorial (click on patent search). Also, patents are available "in search of a business."
www.delphion.com	Quick searches on a specific topic (patent numbers).
www.patentcafe.com	Click on inventors > how-to tutorials > how to patent > inventors starting point > prior art search.
Patent Offices	
www.uspto.gov	Official US patent and trademark office site.
www.patent.gov.uk	For information on British patents.
www.european-patent-office.org	For information on European patents.

This list is by no means exhaustive. Go to any search engine and look up invention, entrepreneurship, innovation, patent search, or creativity and take a journey—a good activity to practice the explorer's mindset. Also use the search engine to explore key words and concepts in the potential problem area or to collect information about an identified topic.

Special recording requirements for inventors

If you are thinking of starting an enterprise based on a new product idea that you want to invent and develop, be aware that inventors are required to document the invention process in an inventor's log. This log has two purposes:

(1) to help you think through and develop ideas, and (2) to protect the completed invention. It thus covers both divergant and convergent thinking. Key features of the log are listed in Table 6.4. The witness should be someone knowledgeable in the area of the invention, but not a relative or close friend.

Table 6.4 *Guidelines for the Inventor's Log*

> ➤ Use a bound notebook and make notes each day about the things you do and learn while working on your invention.
> ➤ Record your idea and how you got it.
> ➤ Write about the problems you have and how you solve them.
> ➤ Write in ink and do not erase.
> ➤ Add sketches and drawings to make things clear.
> ➤ List all parts, sources, and costs of materials.
> ➤ Sign and date all entries at the time they are made and have them witnessed.

Focusing the problem topic

Once you (or your team) have identified a potential problem area or topic, you need to analyze it for size. It will be difficult to generate a good business idea from a topic that is too general or too large. On the other hand, a very narrow topic usually limits the creative possibilities in the solutions that will be generated. If you have a good topic but need to expand the problem, you can ask a series of "what is this about" questions. This technique invites divergent, contextual thinking.

Example of a diverging chain of questions:

"What is this problem about?"

Answer: "Housing."

"What is housing about?"

Answer: "Being warm and cozy."

"What is being warm and cozy about?"

Answer: "Feeling loved, cared for, and safe."

Note how this chain has brought out aspects of the problem that involve not only a physical need but also emotional needs. It helps to get the bigger picture. We must encourage our customers and other people involved with the problem to express the needs or dreams that are important but often remain unspoken.

At other times, to obtain a solution, we have to break problems down into smaller parts through convergent thinking. If we want to '"squeeze" a problem, we can use a chain question process by asking "why?" Such questions can bring out the real reasons why people have a problem or what is important about the problem.

Example of a converging chain of questions:

"Why do you want to improve your budgeting procedure?"

Answer: "Because I'm always late in paying my bills."

"Why are you always late?"

Answer: "Because I have a habit of procrastination."

"Why do you procrastinate?"

Answer: "Because I hate paperwork."

"Why do you hate paperwork?"

Answer: "It requires quadrant B thinking which I hate."

Chain questions let us eliminate rationalization; we can zero in on the real motivation underlying a problem. Here, the real problem is a mismatch between the task and the person's thinking preference, not the budgeting procedure or the habit of procrastination.

TIP: Do not be concerned about selecting just the right size. The problem can be expanded during the idea generation phase by encouraging diverging, wild ideas. If the topic is too broad, it can be broken down into narrower subtopics during idea evaluation.

Using the detective's mindset

Once the "explorer" has identified a tentative problem area, it is time for the "detective" to collect specific information. As "detectives" we search for clues to identify the "real" problem. As seen in Chapter 4, "detectives" ask a lot of questions. In the context of entrepreneurship, a critical factor is the ability to identify your customers and then to ask them the right questions that will give you the information you need for analyzing the problem and making a decision as to the potential of the topic to result in a viable business idea through creative problem solving.

Exercise: What Is the real problem at Algona?

The US Environmental Protection Agency (EPA) has discovered volatile organic compounds in effluents from a processing plant of the Algona Fertilizer Company in

Algona, Iowa. These toxic waste products bypass the city of Algona but are carried into the East Fork of the Des Moines River, a tributary that feeds into Saylorville Lake, the principal source of water for Des Moines, a city of more than 3 million people. The Des Moines city council, through news media and political channels, is putting enormous public pressure on state and federal environmental agencies to shut down the Algona plant. Environmental action groups, with full media coverage, demonstrated yesterday in front of the Iowa governor's mansion to demand immediate closure of the plant. Local TV news and talk shows are starting to focus on the issue. The company's executive board has convened an emergency working group to consider what the company should do.

Every problem, from major ones, such as education and national health care, to mundane ones, such as an overdrawn checking account, can be viewed from multiple conflicting perspectives. And what drives these differing perspectives? Biases and mindsets, those unseen killers of objective truth, determine our perspective on any problem. That perspective, in turn, drives our analysis, our conclusions and rationalizations, and ultimately our recommendations. Another constraint is that the minute we define a problem, our thinking about it quickly narrows considerably, unless we make a determined effort to move from the detective's mindset to the "explorer" or "artist."

Take a moment now and WRITE DOWN here what you think is the "real" problem at Algona. You will miss the full benefits of this exercise if you do not write down your ideas. _____

_____

_____

_____

_____

_____

_____

_____

_____

_____

_____

_____

_____

Now think about the different customers connected to this problem and jot down your ideas. Can you identify at least ten different interest groups or "customers"? Again, write down your answers.

_____
_____
_____
_____
_____
_____
_____
_____
_____
_____
_____
_____
_____
_____

What do you think is the "real" problem now? Has looking at the perspective of different groups given you insight into aspects of the problem you did not consider before? Write a revised problem definition statement that takes your new viewpoint into account. _____

_____
_____
_____
_____
_____
_____
_____
_____
_____
_____
_____

People spend huge amounts of time and effort trying to start a business. Although our advice and exercises take time to apply in practice, this will be time well spent because it will help avoid wasting time in coping with the consequences of making avoidable mistakes. Don't rush it if you are serious.

Asking questions with a customer survey

You may be able to find previously published customer surveys that relate to your proble—as for example in census publications. However, it is more likely, since you are seeking to identify a previously neglected market niche that no previous information exists. Thus you need to develop your own customer survey form. The survey can focus on problems (negatives), or it can focus on desired features and preferences (positives). Tips on how to design a survey of user needs or customer wants are given in Table 6.5 (from Ref. 3.5). Other tools for collecting user needs data suitable for your purpose may be focus groups, telephone interviews, or simple observation of buying preferences.

Table 6.5 *Survey of User Needs*

Address the respondent. Thank the respondent for taking the time to complete the survey. Explain how the survey results will be used and whether they will be anonymous.

Configure for easy scoring. If possible, place the answer blocks directly on the question sheet. Try to keep the survey to one page; at the most, use the front and back of the same page.

Obtain needed demographics. This data can alert you to a non-representative sample group or confirm that it is representative. You may ask for sex, postal code, age range, family income, owned or rented housing, level of education, etc. Be aware, however, that some questions, such as age or family income, may be very sensitive. Ask only what you really need to know to help you make decisions about your planned enterprise. Avoid a data swamp.

Obtain user opinions or preferences. Ask each question in a way that maximizes the information obtained and minimizes the chance of misunderstandings. Ask as few questions as possible to get the needed information.

Example:
1. Do you usually buy electronic Christmas gifts?
2. Do you personally prefer clock radios with CDs or with cassettes?

Improved version:
1. Last Christmas, approximately how much did you spend (total) for electronic gifts? $_____
2. About how much would you be willing to pay for each of the following radios for your own use, if all have equal high-quality sound and tuning capability? Check only one in each row.

	<$20	$20-39	$40-79	$80-119	>$120
Simple AM/FM clock radio	____	____	____	____	____
Clock radio with CD	____	____	____	____	____
Clock radio with cassette	____	____	____	____	____
Clock radio with CD+cassette	____	____	____	____	____

The survey can collect different types of information, either purely quantitative data, or "weighted" data—where people (for each question) can indicate not only if they have a problem but how severe the problem is by ranking it as 0 for no problem, 1 for a small problem, 2 for a moderate problem, and 3 for a severe problem. A similar ranking can be done for preferences. The replies can be tabulated as total points, or they can be stratified into the number of answers for each severity level or strength of preference. Stratified data collection can give better insight. If possible, use a team to design the survey form.

Producing and administering effective survey instruments is a complex task fraught with possibilities of error, both in their design and in the interpretation of results. Piloting new surveys on small samples of the population can help avoid some of these errors. Even deciding on the appropriate population to be surveyed merits considerable thought, especially if stratification of the population, whether intended or not, may bias conclusions derived from the sample. The sample size depends on the level of uncertainty that will satisfy you. For sampling errors of 5 percent, appropriate sample sizes would be 80, 278, 370, and 384 for populations of 100, 1000, 10,000 and essentially infinite, respectively (Ref. 3.5). You should also be aware that a typical response rate to a survey may be less than 15 percent.

Even if you think you already know the needs of a typical user, some minimal survey is usually very useful. In particular, if you are inventing or designing a product that you would like to use, considering yourself as typical of other users in the market invites gross misjudgment. Keep in mind that the goal of a "positive" user survey is to produce a list of desired features ranked according to preference—these are the users' definition of quality for the product (or service)!

Tips and sources of help for customer surveys

A search for "customer surveys" using an Internet search engine will yield an immense number of responses. Among these are software tools for designing surveys, consultant firms, books, on-line newsletters, and sample questions. Ken Miller, at www.adamssixsigma.com/Newsletters/design_redesign.htm, recommends that most customer surveys could be greatly improved if they focused on asking:

- What is expected or wanted in the product or service?
- What was experienced with similar (or your) products or services?
- What is the customer's level of satisfaction with the product/service?

The following common problems with customer surveys were identified:

- The wrong people are surveyed.
- The wrong questions were asked.
- The questions were asked the wrong way.
- The questions are asked at the wrong time.
- Satisfaction and dissatisfaction are assumed to be equally important.
- Those who did not buy or use the product/service are not surveyed.
- Surveys are conducted for the wrong reasons.
- The results are generalized to groups not surveyed.
- Surveys are used as a substitute for better methods.

TIP: A reliance on this kind of wrong information on the "voice of the customer" in shaping your decisions for developing a certain product or service can leave you worse off than if you had no information at all. Thus make sure you expend the necessary care to obtain reliable data (based on a good understanding of statistics) that you can actually use.

Data analysis and the Pareto diagram

It is important to summarize the results of the collected data and record it in the problem briefing. The ranked frequency of identified problems or causes of problems can be effectively visualized in the form of a Pareto diagram. A Pareto diagram is a specialized bar graph used to identify and separate the most important causes of trouble from the more trivial items—those that must be addressed with creative problem solving. The vertical axis can be expressed in numbers or percentage of cases or in terms of the money lost due to the identified defects. For example, in a survey that investigated problems with toasters, it was found that two out of 80 toasters surveyed started a house fire. Even though the number of incidences is low percentage-wise, the costs and seriousness of the damage caused were significant and made this a prime target for problem solving.

Vilfredo Pareto, an Italian economist, invented the diagram. He was struck by the fact that approximately 20 percent of the population in a country commonly controlled 80 percent of the wealth. This 80/20 principle makes it possible to concentrate resources on removing the top 20 percent of causes and thus cure 80 percent of the problems. The Pareto diagram is thus very useful for assigning priorities for continuous improvement. For example, an analysis of problems with curling irons conducted by engineering students at Michigan State University showed that solving the top three flaws would cure 83% of the problems, as shown in Figure 6.2.

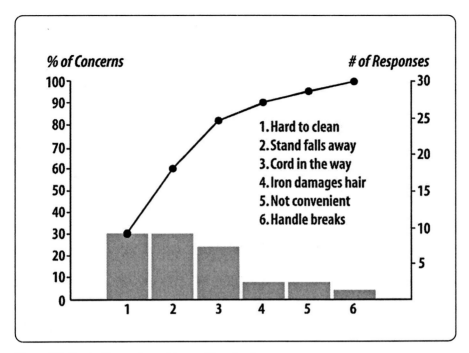

% of Concerns

# of Responses

1. Hard to clean
2. Stand falls away
3. Cord in the way
4. Iron damages hair
5. Not convenient
6. Handle breaks

Figure 6.2 *Pareto diagram for problems with curling irons*

Identifying the "real" problem

Once a problem has been identified, it becomes important to discover the root causes that apply. Many apparent problems are simply symptoms of a deeper condition. Consider the problem of e-mail overload. At face value it might appear that too many people want to communicate with you through e-mail. However, a deeper inquiry into the root causes of e-mail overload would identify ease of access, convenience and the ability to pass on tasks and responsibilities with impunity as the real causes. Lazy people do not want to make a judgment on which trivial information could be useful to whom, so it is sent to all. Also, a substantial report or document that would have had limited circulation due to printing and shipping costs can now be circulated widely for comment. If problems arise later, the authors in defense can cite this wider circulation.

Identifying the "real" customers

In a survey of potential users of a silent signaling device for incoming telephone calls discovered, as expected, a high degree of interest among older people, since many suffer from some degree of hearing loss. But unexpectedly, the survey also found a high preference among office staff personnel who sought relief from the constant ringing of telephones.

The purchaser and the end user are frequently not the same person; thus the business concept must be geared to be attractive to both. Obvious examples are products for children that are purchased by the parents. Services for the elderly (who are the primary users) are often paid for by social services, family members, or insurance companies, and thus the quality of the solution must appeal to a broad range of stakeholders which may not be apparent at first glance. Questionnaires can be designed to bring out these aspects. Also, give some thoughts if you will primarily sell to other businesses, or if you need to attract walk-in or drive-by customers from the general public. Your choice of business location will be important in the latter case, and you may need to conduct some "traffic" surveys and interviews with different local businesses to get a feel for the areas under consideration.

Final tips for problem definition

1. Before moving on to brainstorm possible solutions to a problem, it is crucial that both mindsets be used—the "explorer" to discover the broader context and the "detective" to uncover the root causes involved. Opportunities for new ventures can often be found in areas of weakness of existing products. Much wasted effort can be avoided later by a thorough investigation at this early stage.

2. If you have found several promising or challenging problem areas, you may want to do a brief Pugh method evaluation at this early stage to find the one you (or your team) want to concentrate on. However, successful entrepreneurs have found that it might be better to work with several ideas quickly and to make the final decision later in the creative problem solving process (for instance after the creative idea evaluation stage) when more data on the potential products, concepts and markets are available.

3. Make sure you have included a preliminary patent search to avoid "reinventing the wheel." Although it is possible to work on developing improvements over an existing product, future profitability is usually much higher with a new product that meets an identified market need or niche.

4. Once you have completed the "explorer" and "detective" tasks, it is a simple matter to summarize the collected information in a one-page briefing and to prepare a concise problem definition statement that will guide the direction of idea generation toward better potential solutions and marketable products as discussed in Chapter 4.

Chapter 7
Idea Generation and Patent Protection

In this chapter, we want to elaborate on the artist's mindset with illustrations of some useful tools that can enhance brainstorming, such as the creative thinking warm-up and some force-fitting or throught-starter tools. The topic of intellectual property protection with a focus on patents is discussed in some detail with practical information, and several useful Internet links and tips for inventors and entrepreneurs given as well.

Using the artist's mindset

Characteristics of the artist's mindset were described in Chapter 4, followed by the procedure of how to conduct a classical brainstorming session. Here, we will elaborate on or illustrate three tools that can be used to enhance brainstorming. In addition, playing around with creative ideas is one way for us to exercise our brain in looking at things "differently"—and one interesting database to explore and mine for all kinds of ideas are existing patents ranging from "wacky" to extremely useful and profitable.

Example of a creative thinking warm-up

Brainstorming is not used just once in the process of becoming an entrepreneur and starting your own business. It is a tool to be used each time you are looking for more than one alternative, from identifying a customer need or market niche (as "explorers" and "detectives") to coming up with ideas for meeting the need, then finding the best approach to produce, and marketing the best idea, service or product.

Most people will dive right into brainstorming. The process can be made more effective when a creative thinking warm-up is used. This allows the participants to switch mentally away from other tasks they may have been involved in that day, especially if these were worrisome or heavily involved left-brain thinking modes. It also facilitates the transition from the problem briefing (mostly quadrant A information) and instructions on the procedure to be used in the actual brainstorming process (mostly quadrant B process) to the freewheeling, expressive right-brain thinking needed for generating creative and innovative ideas.

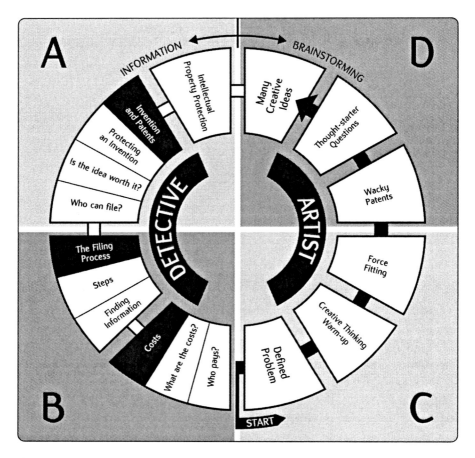

Figure 7.1 *Thinking tasks and just-in-time learning for generating ideas & protecting your intellectual property (superimposed on the four-quadrant ABCD model developed by Ned Herrmann)*

For the creative thinking warmup, you may use a flip chart or wall board to quickly jot down the warm-up ideas as they are called out. A small group may be warmed-up with twenty ideas—a larger, analytically minded group may take longer. Once unusual and funny ideas are brought forth and the group begins to laugh, the warm-up has succeeded and the regular brainstorming can begin immediately.

Table 7.1 lists the ideas from a lengthy warm-up using a one-foot square of aluminum foil as the object. Note that an occasional "crazy" idea may appear early in the process, but it usually takes some time for the participants to purge their minds of the practical and mundane ideas before they become more daring, exploratory and humorous.

Table 7.1 *Fifty Uses for a Square of Aluminum Foil*

1 Wrap food for freezer	2 Cook (bake) food in it
3 Wrap for package/sandwich	4 Pie pan or candy mold
5 Emergency drinking cup	6 Holder for sticky object
7 Use as lid	8 Funnel
9 Table mat	10 Cake decorating tool
11 Grill cover	12 Scrub rust from metal tools
13 Drip pan liner	14 Emergency gas cap for car
15 Shelf liner	16 Protector for dripping candles
17 Gift wrap	18 Airflow deflector
19 Ball or toy animals	20 Sun reflector/signaling device
21 Window shade	22 Shade for transplanted seedlings
23 Scarecrow	24 Wrap for small flower bouquet
25 Vent cover	26 Stuffing for drafts/holes in walls
27 Bird cage liner	28 Catch water under flower pot
29 Picture frame	30 Garbage bag for "yucky" stuff
31 Shelf liner	32 Emergency purse for small items
33 Creative art material	34 Christmas decoration or craft
35 Make jewelry	36 Make a relief print or "rubbing"
37 Shower cap	38 Punch holes to make sifter
39 Make play money	40 Put into shoe for temporary repair
41 Fold into artful bookmark	42 Shoe shield for walking in mud
43 Silver confetti/tinsel	44 Angel halo for Christmas pageant
45 Eye mask during carnival	46 Roll up, use to blow soap bubbles
47 Tin man costume for doll	48 Book cover for "silver" library
49 Mouse suit	50 Boat for beetles or bugs or slugs

Examples of force fitting

When we put two unrelated ideas together and try to make them fit, this mental exercise help us to generate new and especially creative ideas. This exercise can be used to energize a sluggish brainstorming session. The process can also be used to improve and hitchhike on ideas that have already been posted (for example during brainstorming or during the Pugh method evaluation in the engineer's mindset).

Example 1: Use the idea of caged white rats to improve business in a travel agency.
- Have a wild-animal decorating scheme (including live animals from a featured tour-of-the-month exotic location).
- Use a white rat escaping from a cage as the logo, as the agency features special trips to escape the "rat race."

- Special promotion of trips to the zoo (with low rates for kids).
- Have the staff dress up in white rat costumes and form a band.
- Feature special science tours to study some endangered species or ecological niche, or sponsor an environmental cleanup (locally or at an interesting travel location).

Can you see how different aspects of the two unrelated ideas lead to creative as well as practical ideas?

Example 2: Combine the two ideas of soap and paper.
- Paper soap; soap paper (noun-noun combination).
- Soapy paper; papery soap (adjective-noun combination).
- Soap *wets* paper; soap *cleans* paper, soap *smoothes* paper (verbs).

Then each of these concepts can be used as a trigger for creative ideas, depending on the original problem. In this example, this approach could lead to some innovative ideas if your problem was to find a new way of packaging soap.

Example of a wacky patent

For a good laugh, a creative thinking warm-up, and to learn what NOT to patent, see **www.colitz.com/site/wacky.htm**. Click on "Wacky Patent of the Month" or "Prior Wacky Patent." An example is given in Figure 7.2.

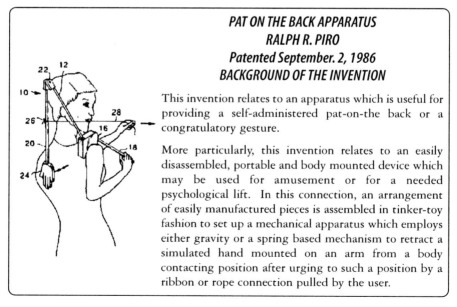

PAT ON THE BACK APPARATUS
RALPH R. PIRO
Patented September. 2, 1986
BACKGROUND OF THE INVENTION

This invention relates to an apparatus which is useful for providing a self-administered pat-on-the back or a congratulatory gesture.

More particularly, this invention relates to an easily disassembled, portable and body mounted device which may be used for amusement or for a needed psychological lift. In this connection, an arrangement of easily manufactured pieces is assembled in tinker-toy fashion to set up a mechanical apparatus which employs either gravity or a spring based mechanism to retract a simulated hand mounted on an arm from a body contacting position after urging to such a position by a ribbon or rope connection pulled by the user.

Figure 7.2 *Wacky patent of the month (Jan. 1998, US Patent No. 4,608,967)*

Example of a thought-starter tool

Table 7.2 is an example of a thought-starter tool designed to help people generate creative ideas. The acronym SCAMPER will remind you of this list. A number of idea-generating tools have been developed based on this list and are available commercially as hand-held tools, wallet-size tables, decks of cards, large wall charts, or software packages. They are just different ways of asking what if and what else.

***Table 7.2** Dr. Osborn's Nine Thought-Starter Questions*

1. **Substitute?** Who else? What else instead? Other place? Other time? Other tone of voice? Other ingredient? Other material? Other process? Other power source? Other approach?

2. **Combine?** How about a blend, assortment, alloy, ensemble? Combine ideas, appeals or purposes? Combine units? Combine functions?

3. **Adapt?** What else is like this? What other idea does this suggest? Any idea in the past that could be copied or adapted?

4. **Magnify?** What to add? Greater frequency? Stronger? Larger? Higher? Longer? Thicker? Extra value? "Plus" ingredient? Multiply? Exaggerate?

5. **Modify?** Change meaning, color, motion, sound, odor, taste, form, shape, or texture? Other changes? New twist?

6. **Put to other uses?** New ways to use object as is? Other uses or purpose if modified?

7. **Eliminate?** What to subtract? Smaller? Lighter? Slower? Split up? Less frequent? Condense? Miniaturize? Minify? Streamline? Understate? Simplify?

8. **Rearrange?** Other layout? Other sequence? Change pace? Other pattern? Change schedule? Transpose cause and effect?

9. **Reverse?** Opposites? Turn it backward? Transpose positive and negative? Mirror-reverse it? Turn it upside down or inside out?

Types of intellectual property protection

Let us say that your use of the creative problem solving process resulted in a very exciting and novel idea. So this is the time you may want to start thinking about what steps you should take to protect your idea. The form of protection depends on the type of intellectual property as listed in Table 7.3. The following information applies to US laws and conditions—patent protection is different in different countries!

Table 7.3 *Types of Intellectual Property*

TYPE OF ASSET	TYPE OF PROTECTION
Invention	Patent
Logo or mark	Trademark
Physical expression of information	Copyright (i.e., book)
Technology/marketing information	Trade secret

What is a patent?

A utility patent protects processes, machines, articles of manufacturing, and compositions of matter for 20 years. A design patent protects ornamental designs for manufactured articles for 14 years. The idea must be novel and non-obvious. A patent protects the right of the inventor(s) to exclude others from making, using or selling the claimed invention or design during the term of the patent in exchange for public disclosure of the invention when the patent is granted. The patent can be licensed to another person or company. Patent rights are enforced by lawsuits in US federal court to prevent infringement by unauthorized making, using, or selling.

What is a trademark?

A trademark can be words, names, symbols, and other devices to distinguish goods or services. The first user of the trademark can obtain protection. The mark is protected when it is registered by the US Patent and Trademarks Office and used on goods and services. It is protected for an initial 10 years and renewable for additional 10-year terms. The trademark protects the right to stop others from using similar trademarks that might cause confusion or deception regarding the protected item.

What is a copyright?

Writings, music, and works of art that have been reduced to a tangible medium of expression (such as in books, audio tapes, video tapes, software) can be copyrighted. The subject matter must be an original creation—not copied— and the copyright notice must be applied when published. The originators of the work hold the copyright, but it can be assigned to others. The copyright holders need to apply to the Copyright Office for a registration certificate. Protection lasts for the life of the author plus 50 years for works created after 1977, and it grants the right to stop others from copying protected work unless granted permission by the copyright holder. Note that the materials can be used —only the unauthorized copying constitutes an infringement on the copyright.

What is a trade secret?

A trade secret can be a formula, pattern, customer list, device, program, or any other compilation of information. These items do not have to be patentable. A trade secret must be kept secret (through established internal and external security measures) and must be used in a business to give an advantage over others who do not know or use it. President Clinton signed the Economic Espionage Act of 1996 into law. Any person converting a trade secret to his or her own benefit commits an act of trade secret theft which is now a federal criminal offense. Also, civil courts can grant injunctions to prevent ex-employees from working for competitors when a strong likelihood of trade secret disclosure exists, even if this might be unintentional or subconscious.

Invention and patents

Entrepreneurs most likely want to seek intellectual property protection for inventions that they plan to sell (license or manufacture and market). Thus the next group of questions relate specifically to inventions, followed by questions about the patent filing process.

What can you do to protect your invention?

• Make sure your invention is novel and practical (or useful). It does not have to be an entirely new idea; it can be an improvement over an existing patent.

• Keep records that carefully document your discovery; be secretive at this point. If you do not have proof of the date of your invention, your patent may be invalidated.

• Carefully search and study existing literature and patents relating to your invention.

• If possible, make a prototype that works.

• Prepare and file a description of your invention.

• Be patient. It takes two years to process a patent. It is also usual for the patent examiner to reject the initial application. You then must overcome the objections.

What are some common mistakes to avoid with inventions?

• Talking without protection (use signed non-disclosure forms).

• Poor prior art search.

• Leaving out claims that others can work around—a patent lawyer can be useful for carefully determining and expanding the areas of your claims.

- Selfishness—not rewarding or including co-inventors.

- Filing too many patents.

- Filing in too many countries.

- Assuming a US patent affords world-wide protection.

- Assuming patent laws are the same around the world. For example, before telling anyone or using the invention in public anywhere in the world, the UK inventor must obtain confidentiality agreements from anyone to whom the invention is revealed in part or in full for development purposes. In the US, disclosure of an invention is OK if the patent application is filed within one year of invention.

- Assuming that all developed countries have the same degree of respect for intellectual property.

- Forgetting that the patent application will be published 18 months after filing, under the Patent Cooperation Treaty.

What if you want to keep your idea a secret?

Not all inventions are patented. You may have some valid reasons for keeping your invention a secret and for wanting to save the costs of obtaining a patent. Trade secret protection might be the better choice if you are sure you want to go into business by yourself, will only have a few people involved in the process, your idea would be difficult to copy, and you will be dealing with a rapidly changing product or market.

How do you know you have an idea worth patenting?

Once you have completed the evaluation and judgment phases in creative problem solving (including the Pugh method with some market analysis), you will have a fair idea about the merits of your invention. Chapter 8 will discuss several sources and processes that can help you evaluate your idea or product.

Important inventions are not always complicated, high-tech products invented by scientists and engineers. Sometimes, an invention has to wait for technological development (or another invention) before it becomes widely adopted—the can opener was invented 50 years after the first tin can was used to conserve food. Interesting information about different categories of inventors (including black, Canadian, Chinese, women, and young) can be found at **www.inventors.about.com/library**. This is just one example of a commercial website, and the viewer must be aware that such information may not be accurate or complete. Do not use such sites for patent searching; the example site given here is merely to show that anyone can invent something worth patenting. This site also has a "wacky patent" file with several funny subcategories. The odds of making it with your invention are increased substantially if you follow the creative problem solving process in this book.

Who can file for a patent?

In the US, it is the person who invents, keeps an inventor's log, and files a provisional patent—it is the inventor (or group of inventors) that can file for a patent. The inventors need not be US citizens. The requirements may be different in other countries. For example in the UK, the first person to apply for the patent can receive the patent—this can be anyone: inventor, business partner, or sponsor. Patents can be filed by a single inventor or a group of co-inventors (see Table 7.4 on the following page for examples of some famous co-inventors). Sometimes the organization licensing a product becomes more famous (and prosperous) than the original inventor. An example is Dr. Yoshiro Nakamatz, the original inventor of the floppy disk and virtually unknown in the US, although he holds over 2000 patents. Groups of technical people at IBM (including Alan Shugart and Dick Morley) worked on the development of the disk and are usually credited with being its inventors.

The patent filing process

What are the main steps for filing for a patent in the US?

The applicant must make sure to have the date of the conception of the invention protected by either having a witnessed, permanently bound, page-numbered notebook or other notarized records. Once the decision to seek patent protection has been made, the following are the main steps in the process:

1. **A disclosure document** in a standard format is completed and sent to the US Patent and Trademark Office where it is held and preserved for two years (for a small fee).

2. The inventor needs to conduct a thorough **search on patentability**—has the idea (or have any of the possible claims) already been protected by a patent?

3. If the invention has been shown to be original (or novel) and useful, the inventor can then file a **provisional application for a patent**. This establishes the filing date. The application should be as complete as possible but need not include all claims. This will allow the inventor to show "Patent Pending" on the product.

Table 7.4 *Some Interesting Inventions and Inventors*

Earmuffs were invented in 1873 by 13-year-old Chester Greenwood.

Band-Aids were invented by an employee of Johnson & Johnson.

Stephanie Kwolek, a chemist with DuPont, invented the miracle fiber, Kevlar.

The Bobcat loader was invented by Louis Keller, a North Dakota farmer with little education.

Keith D. Elwick of Vinton, Iowa, invented a manure spreader that became so popular in England that Queen Elizabeth II awarded him a silver medal and trophy for his creativity.

Two Hungarian chemists, George and Ladislao Biro, patented the ballpoint pen in 1938.

It took Guideon Sundback 30 years to perfect the slide fastener (zipper) patented in 1913.

Charles F. Nelson invented the mousetrap (Patent No. 661,068).

Patent No. 821,393 for a "Flying Machine" was granted to Orville and Wilbur Wright in 1906.

Bette Graham, a housewife and typist, invented "liquid paper"; her company was sold in 1980 for over $47 million.

Mary Anderson received a patent for windshield wipers in 1903. Josephine Cochrane patented a dishwasher in 1914. Marion Donovan received a patent for the first disposable diaper in 1951. Rose Totino patented a dough for frozen pizza in 1979.

Bernard Silver and Joseph Woodland, two graduate students at Drexel, invented the barcode and received Patent No. 2,612,994 in 1952. Silver died in 1962 before seeing the invention commercialized. President Bush awarded Woodland the 1992 National Medal of Technology. Neither inventor made much money on the idea that started a billion dollar business.

Henry Ford patented a transmission mechanism in 1911 (Patent No. 1,005,186).

George De Mestral was granted a patent for an "Adhesive Element in Cloth Form" in 1973 (Patent No. 3,748,701)—we know it as Velcro.

Marcian Edward Hoff, Stanley Mazor and Frederico Faggin received Patent No. 3,821,715 in 1974 for a "Memory System for Multi-Chip Digital Computer."

---

4. Within 12 months of the application, the inventor must file **a non-provisional application** including a declaration of inventorship. Upon receipt, the application is given a patent serial number and filing date and is then examined by a patent examiner. This application must be complete in all details and include all claims. For this reason, entrepreneurs and inventors with strong quadrant D thinking preferences are urged to seek the help of a patent attorney with quadrant B thinking skills to prepare the patent application. Although it is possible to complete the entire application alone, the risks of leaving out some claims on the patent drawing and application are very great—anything left out leaves the product unprotected.

5. If the patent application is rejected, it can be amended and resubmitted. Check with the US Patent and Trademark Office as to the exact procedures that must be followed.

For more information on US patent law and to obtain the required forms, go to **www.uspto.gov**.

What else should you know about finding information and avoiding scams?

As you can see from Table 7.5, **www.inventnet.com** has a slew of useful information, beginning with *Inventing and Patenting Help*. Be sure to check *Invention Scams* and the separate warning at the head of the InventNET home page. Click on *International Patent Offices* and you will be provided with a list of links to patent offices in many different countries (in their respective languages). Other sources of information are listed in Table 7.6.

Table 7.5 *Main Menu of Available Information from InventNET*

• Inventing and Patenting Help	• Patent Attorney Directory
• Bookstore	• Inventor Trade Shows
• Get Your Free Email	• InventNET Forum
• Invention for Sale	• Patent and Licensing Forms
• Patent Search	• Classifieds
• Invention Scams	• Useful Links
• Prototype Work	• About InventNET
• Products and Services	• International Patent Offices
• Inventor Organizations	• Inventor Organizations

Table 7.6 *Books with Patent Information*

> David Pressman, *Patent It Yourself*, Nolo Press, Berkeley, California, 9th edition, March 2002. This book contains useful hints and forms for those who want to apply for their own patents.
>
> US Department of Commerce: *Patents and How to Get One: A Practical Handbook*. This paperback is listed at **www.amazon.com** for $3.50 and represents a very good value.
>
> Search **www.amazon.com** for "Patents" and then choose among a long list of books for those that fit your particular circumstances and interests (and pocketbook).

Costs

How much does it cost to file for a US patent?

Filing for a patent—the non-provisional application—can be very expensive in the long term. Check with the patent office for the latest pricing information. The costs are typically as follows, if the inventor asserts in writing that he or she is "a small entity" (otherwise the prices are double). The filing fee for a provisional application is $80 and for a utility patent around $400. Maintaining a patent is expensive. At 3-1/2 years, the fee is around $500, at 7-1/2 years, $1000, and at 11-1/2 years, $1600. These high maintenance fees again point out the importance of having an invention with marketability in the near- to medium-term.

What happens when a patent expires?

Many patents expire due to non-payment of the maintenance fee or because the protection limit has been reached. Others can then use the patent in their own inventions.

For example, US Patent No. 2,292,387 for a spread-spectrum communication system originally invented by H.K. Markey and George Antheil (an avant-garde composer) was recently used by another inventor in the Secure ID System (patent pending). H.K. Markey is better known as the Hollywood actress Hedy Lamarr, and the "secret communication system" was intended for launching torpedoes during WWII.

Other current uses are in satellite and cellular telephone communication security. All later spread-spectrum patents acknowledge the original (which was kept classified by the US government until 1985).

> ***There are many do's and dont's in the invention game;***
> ***learn the ropes—dont jump in head first.***
> www.inventNET.com

Who pays for the patent?

A critical issue in the protection of intellectual property concerns payment for patent protection. Often, those who filed for patent protection then claim ownership of the intellectual property involved. It is crucially important to clarify and resolve this issue prior to disclosure and patent application. Consider the following four situations.

1. **University Staff and Students**: Increasingly, universities are being encouraged to develop and exploit their intellectual property. This affects both staff and students. When intellectual property with commercial potential is identified, it may be university policy to process and pay for patent applications centrally. In this case, the university staff member or student involved may lose ownership of the intellectual property. In many places, if you are a staff member or graduate student, you may not have any choice but to turn over ownership to the university. Universities commonly have a person or an office responsible for intellectual property. If the university licenses your invention, you may be entitled to a certain percentage of the royalties. In any case, be very sure you check out your rights.

TIP: The inventors may not have sufficient resources, time, interest, patience, or rights to pursue a patent application. However, they may be able to negotiate a percentage of future royalties. Such amounts are low, since the university is assuming the risk of paying for the patent up front without assurance that the invention will be commercially profitable. Typically, the royalty to the inventor is in the range of 5 to 15% at most.

2. **Employees of Companies**: As with universities, more companies are now actively encouraging the development of intellectual property and its commercialization within the business. Many large companies directly promote such activity by their employees through the specific provision of time and resource for this purpose. Again, it is vital that those who generate new ideas are fully aware of how to retain ownership in the context of the companies' policy and practice in this area.

TIPS: Companies are more likely to pay a cash bonus for a successful invention than to assign a percentage of profits. If the invention was made as part of the regular employment and using the company's resources, little if any special recompense should be expected. However, if the employee has a creative idea and develops it in his or her own time at home (without any of the company's resources), the employee must carefully investigate if independent pursuit of the patent is feasible:

- Is it allowed under company policy? Intellectual property developed by employees may be vulnerable to lawsuits even if generated in the employee's own time, particularly if the idea turns out to be very successful.
- Is the market potential sufficient to warrant the time and costs of seeking a patent?
- Can the employee afford the investment in time and costs?

3.   Government Employees: Employees of national or local government departments may also develop intellectual property that has commercial potential.   Again they should seek information and advice on the most appropriate strategy to adopt and the regulations that apply. Some government agencies (especially those working in the forefront of high technology development), may have some system of recognition or recompense available for their inventors. For example, NASA pays a bonus to employees who obtain patents (but only when the invention has a payback exceeding the cost for getting the patent).

4.   Intellectual Property Protection for Entrepreneurs: The observations and warnings provided above should also be kept in mind by individual entrepreneurs. If you have checked out some of the information on the patenting process given on the recommended web sites, you will be aware that the decision about going forward with a patent application requires serious thought. Professional advice should be obtained to ascertain the most economical and appropriate way of proceeding before simply applying for patents as a matter of course or a matter of pride.

Chapter 8
Developing a "Best" Solution

In this chapter, we want to elaborate on some of the assessment activities that occur concurrently during the Pugh evaluation process. We saw in Chapter 5 that the Pugh method helps us distill a "best" or optimal solution from several distinctly different original concepts. The "engineer" is the primary mindset, aided by the "judge" for analysis and the "artist" for additional creative thinking. The thinking tasks involved in moving from the initial brainstormed ideas to a final concept or product—which, when built, results in a prototype that confirms this best design— are shown in the double "wheel" of Figure 8.1. The outer path indicates the Phase 1 rounds of the Pugh method, and the inner path represents the Phase 2 rounds.

Pugh method Phase 1: Developing better ideas

To make it easier to develop different concepts for the Pugh evaluation, it is recommended that the many ideas that came out of the first brainstorming be processed in a round of creative idea evaluation—essentially a second round of brainstorming using the engineer's mindset—as discussed in Chapter 4. Depending on the problem topic, the outcome of this will be either a smaller number of better, more practical ideas, or a list of design criteria or goals that the solution or new product must meet to satisfy customer needs.

Evaluation criteria

The first item needed for the Pugh evaluation matrix is a set of valid evaluation criteria. Brainstorm a list of criteria and then narrow the list down to about twenty of the most important items. These criteria address all important customer needs and the concerns of all stakeholders. As was shown with "The Problem at Algona," a problem rarely involves only one customer. In a manufactured product, the end user is only one customer—let's say a child in the case of a juvenile car safety seat. Other customers would be the purchaser (likely a parent), the retailer or store manager, the seat manufacturer and the carmakers, insurance companies, and perhaps repair persons as well as law enforcement and emergency personnel, and finally society (for the recycling and other environmental aspects in addition to general child welfare and safety concerns).

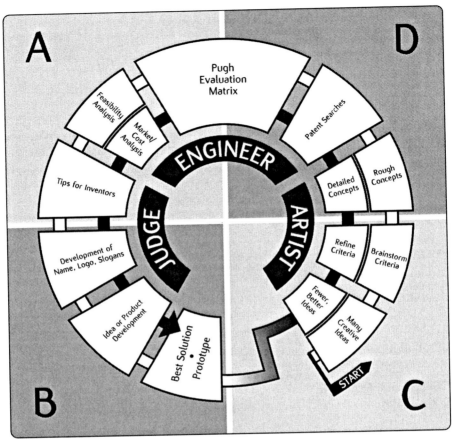

Figure 8.1 *Thinking tasks and just-in-time learning for developing creative concepts and synthesizing a "best" solution (superimposed on four-quadrant ABCD model developed by Ned Herrmann)*

Developing different concepts or designs

Based on the problem briefing and an understanding of the problem-solving goal, use the brainstormed ideas to work out several distinct solutions. They need not be perfect at this point, but each concept should constitute a creative approach for solving the problem. Each concept should be worked out to about the same level of detail. For designs, prepare a large sketch that shows the major features of the product. For services, solutions and other intangible options, prepare a condensed description of the major features and post each concept on a flip chart page. There should be a minimum of three or four alternatives as a start—more will be generated as the process continues. In a design team, it is often expedient to have each team member develop a separate idea or concept.

Other types of evaluation teams can of course take this approach. Again, we want to emphasize that it is very important to use the artist's mindset at this stage to generate very creative ideas; the natural process of evaluation with critical thinking will tend to make these concepts more practical in later rounds.

Patent searches

Phase 1 patent searches can be idea starters as you develop different concepts. They can be applied to the entire concept or just to certain parts or features. Since about 80 percent of patents are not entirely original but constitute improvements of existing patents, this can be a source of good ideas for your concepts, either by adding practical aspects, or by prompting your mind to make a creative leap through force-fitting or overcoming some "ridiculous" idea. During Phase 2, patent searches should become more focused in the area of the emerging winning solutions.

Evaluation matrix and reviews

Using the brainstormed criteria and the initial concepts, set up the evaluation matrix and conduct the evaluation as discussed in Chapter 5. Then review the results and continue to improve the concepts in two or more rounds, with the highest-scoring concept chosen as the datum for each subsequent matrix.

Preliminary analyses

Toward the end of Phase 1, several analyses can be conducted on the highest-ranking ideas to help judge the merit of the different options, including technical analysis, feasibility, and initial market analysis.

Technical Analysis

The proposed concepts should be analyzed as to their technical aspects. Does the concept use existing technology? Can it be used as is? Will it have to be modified? Will it have to be purchased? Is it protected by a patent? Does it need development? If yes, what is the time line? What would be the costs? What would be the competitive advantages? What are the trends—is rapid change expected, and how would this affect you?

This analysis may point out three options, where one definitely involves a long-term view:

- Go with existing technology.
- Go with existing technology, with adaptations.
- Go with existing technology, while simultaneously working on developing an advanced concept to maintain or expand the future market for your product or business.

Thus this analysis can point out the most promising areas for R&D investments for your business.

Feasibility Analysis

This involves the whole context of what you want to do with the "best" idea once you have developed it, from business planning to obtaining financing and ethics. A number of these aspects will be discussed in Chapters 9 and 10. At this point, you merely need to have a rough yet realistic estimate of the scope of your potential enterprise and if it appears to be doable.

Initial Market Analysis

All the work you have done in developing an invention or other business idea will come to naught if you give little thought to the market. Who will buy your product or pay for your idea? What will be your profits after you have paid for all your expenses? Chapter 8 will present some questionnaires and assessment tools that will help you think through marketing questions.

After two or three rounds of the Pugh method, you and your team will begin to have a fair idea on the strengths (and weaknesses) of your ideas and concepts. You may want to check out the market potential with a typical sample of customers—information on survey forms was given in Chapter 7. If you have made an invention and your research has shown that nothing like this is being sold anywhere, could the reason be that you have come up with a breakthrough idea or that there is simply no market or interest in your idea? Critically evaluate these two possibilities, without personal bias or blind spots. An ideal situation would be a market where potential customers show interest but have no other loyalties or brand preferences.

You can begin your search for market information on the Internet and in public libraries (looking for special reports on markets in your product area in business magazines, for example). A very structured, highly competitive market is difficult to enter, whereas a fragmented or emerging market may have many niches that can be filled with new products. Keep in mind that having a lot of published information available about a market's potential also means shrinking opportunity because many competitors can be expected to enter such a market.

> **As a rule of thumb, the product's selling price should be three to five times its manufacturing cost, or you will be unlikely to make a profit.**

Pugh method Phase 2: Converging to a "best" solution

In the rounds of Phase 1, you and your team have most likely come up with a several additional ideas or concepts. In Phase 2, you will begin dropping the weakest concepts and more fully develop the stronger solutions. Eventually, the process will converge to a single, "best" or optimal solution that is supported by the entire team. However, to be able to judge the merits of different concepts that remain in the running toward the end, it will be advantageous to conduct additional analyses.

Refining the evaluation criteria

Not just the concepts, but also the criteria, are being developed and refined during Phase 2, both based on the discussion during the completion of each evaluation matrix and data obtained from the analyses being done.

Developing improved and more detailed concepts

In each round, the concepts are worked out in more detail (with data from the technical and cost analyses, as well as from input from potential customers). In some projects, you may not have time to continue the process until you have convergence to a single, best solution. In this case, it will be especially important to supplement your evaluation with data from the Phase 2 analyses.

Evaluation matrix and documentation

It is important that a careful record be maintained of the results of each evaluation, as well as of the descriptions or drawings of each concept being evaluated, together with notes on the evaluation process and discussions. Also record the rationale why particular concepts are being discarded.

Additional analyses

Three different types of analyses are very helpful to determine the merit of the final ideas: (a) a detailed market analysis including research, (b) an an analysis of costs (for development, manufacturing, and marketing of the product), (c) a risk and resource analysis.

A GOOD MARKETING STRATEGY RESTS ON THREE KEY ELEMENTS
- ➤ *Know yourself.*
- ➤ *Know your customers—their likes, dislikes and expectations.*
- ➤ *Know your competitors—their strengths and weaknesses.*

Detailed Market Research and Analysis

If you have not explored these areas during the problem definition phase, start your market research by making a list of different categories that might be related to your concept or product (where the "product" can be a service). These are called research fields. Get ideas for fields by:

- Searching through different companies on the web
- Looking through catalogues of related products
- Visiting stores
- Talking to experts
- Attending trade shows—the offerings are vast.

For your idea to have market value, you must determine the following:

- Will your invention (product or process) work as intended?
- What is the competition? If there is no competition, BEWARE!
- Is there a need for this product?
- What future changes, trends, or sudden paradigm shifts could affect demand for your product?

For some inventions, there is no question of the value (such as a vaccine to eradicate a deadly disease). But for many products, you will have to create a market (as was the case, for example, for the Post-it notes). From the Pugh method, you will gain a clear idea of

> *Great devices are created by engineers, great products are created by marketing.*
>
> Peter Drucker

the customer benefits: Does your idea perform a task that has not been achieved before, or can it do the task faster, better, easier, or at substantially lower cost?

Chapter 9 includes a questionnaire for developing a marketing plan. Right now, Table 8.1 lists some initial questions that you need to answer to gain an understanding of the market conditions your product will face. If your answers are different from those indicated, evaluate why and investigate how the obstacle can be overcome with additional problem solving as you develop your concepts.

Analysis of Development, Manufacturing, and Marketing Costs

It will be very helpful at this stage to prepare a realistic estimate of the development, manufacturing and marketing costs, especially of you are comparing two or three good but very different "better" concepts. Your final decision on which product to choose for your enterprise will have to weigh these costs against your available resources and the level of risk you can live with.

Chapter 9 includes guidelines on how to assess the profit potential of your "best" idea or product emerging at the end of the Phase 2 Pugh evaluation.

Table 8.1 *Self-Assessment Questions Related to the Market*

Competition	
1. Are similar products or ideas already on the market *(conduct a product search)?*	No
2. Are there previous relevant patents or patent applications *(conduct a patent search)?*	No
3. Is the market very competitive for these types of products?	No
4. Could competitors quickly catch up and take a substantial market share?	No
5. Can you effectively compete in price, quality, and service?	Yes
6. Are your product's features unique?	Yes
7. Are your product's benefits obvious?	Yes
8. Does your product provide more customer choice and value?	Yes
9. Will increased competition affect your profit level negatively?	No
Market	
1. Do you know who the customers will be and the size of the market— local, regional, global; private, industry, commerce, wholesale, retail, government, etc?	Yes
2. Will the product or service by in constant demand?	Yes
3. For something entirely new, can you create a demand for the service or product?	Yes
4. Is the potential market likely to grow? How fast?	Yes
5. Are there additional applications for your product?	Yes
6. Is your idea filling a market gap (open door) by meeting a clear customer need?	Yes
7. Will your market be immune to overall economic conditions?	Yes
8. Could an existing company introduce your idea with a better chance of success? *(If yes, consider licensing your idea to them.)*	Yes/No
9. Are there legal, regulatory, environmental or other factors hindering market entry?	No

Risk and Resource Analysis

Table 8.2 gives some self-assessment questions regarding manufacturing risk and resource requirements. If you can answer all the resource questions in the affirmative, your risks will be relatively low. The majority of new businesses start with an initial investment of less than $10,000; thus only a modest investment is at stake should the enterprise fail (and the value of what can be learned from the "failure" may far outweigh this initial loss if it forms the stepping stone to a successful business later).

Table 8.2 *Self-Assessment Questions Related to Risk and Resources*

Risk

1. Is innovative technology needed for producing the idea? *The more innovative the technology, the bigger the risk to the manufacturer.*

2. Is the idea a new application of an existing product or process? *This may be less risky.*

3. Does your idea depend on at least one other innovation being operational before it can be successful? *This dependency vastly increases the risk.*

4. Will the product be cheaper when produced in larger volumes? *The higher initial costs increase the initial risk.*

5. Is the technology involved relatively simple? *The risks are lower.*

6. Are several complex systems integrated in your innovation? *This will increase the risk.*

7. Do you have a working prototype? *This decreases the risk as well as the development costs.*

Resources

1. Can you fully develop and exploit your idea with little or no additional resources and investment?

2. Can you start exploitation with few resources and expand later?

3. Can your idea be implemented quickly (in less than two years)?

4. Are external funds available for development?

5. Can you do the development yourself, preferably with little additional training?

6. Are you able to obtain assistance from people with know-how at reasonable cost if needed?

7. Will you be able to cope with short-term ups and downs?

8. Will patent protection for your product outweigh the costs?

9. Will your product be easy to distribute (at low cost)?

IMPORTANT TIP:
Dont think invention—
THINK BUSINESS OPPORTUNITY!

Special tips for entrepreneurial inventors

If your product is an invention, does it meet most of the criteria for a successful invention listed in Table 8.3? These tips for inventors were prepared by the National Endowment for Science, Technology and the Arts (NESTA) in the UK.

Table 8.3 *When You Invent—Strategies for Success*

- Don't expect anyone to beat a path to your door (unless they intend to rip you off). Good things will happen only if you get out there and make them happen.

- Companies often complain that inventors aren't on their wavelength. To you, your idea is your baby, precious and unique. To companies it's just another log on the fire. Swallow whatever it is you need to swallow and get on the other party's wavelength.

- Innovation brings rewards but it also brings risks, so ALWAYS control your costs and ALWAYS limit your risk.

- A typical development time scale is two to three years—often more and rarely less—so plan carefully and never rush into anything.

- Learn continuously, especially about the market and/or companies you're aiming for. You'll get lots of conflicting advice along the way, so you need a good store of knowledge to make sound judgments.

- Be as professional as you can in all your dealings. Claiming that because you're more of a creative type it's okay to be disorganized, unreliable and inflexible just won't wash.

- No matter how highly you rate your own abilities you won't be able to do everything on your own, so be prepared to be part of a team that shares the work and the spoils fairly.

- In the interest of self-preservation, regard being an inventor as a short-term job with a limited aim: to develop your idea only to the point where potential licensees, partners, investors or buyers can clearly judge its commercial worth.

- Beyond that point, either back off and leave the licensees to get on with it or—if it's your own business—forget being an inventor and go full tilt for entrepreneurial success.

We want to bring this chapter (and the Pugh method evauluation) to a close with a brief overview of three topics: creating a product name or a business logo, product development, and prototyping.

Name selection and protection

The Pugh method evaluations may also give you some good ideas for a creative name for your product and possibly a memorable logo for your business. In the early rounds, you can play around with several ideas, and you can come up with interesting, original, and descriptive names for each of the concepts being evaluated.

Product Name

Once you have identified or developed the "best" concept or product, use the creative problem solving process to brainstorm and develop a definitive name for your product. Do not underestimate the importance of the product's name. Sometimes, the name as an asset can be more valuable than the product itself. You will have to check and make sure that the name you have selected is not already "owned" by someone else and protected by a trademark. Then you will have to take steps to register your trademark, so it will be protected. Even if you are not planning to manufacture or market your own product (preferring to license it instead), an interesting name as a "hook" may spark the interest of a large company to where you will have a chance to make a sales presentation.

Business Name and Logo

As soon as you have a fair understanding about the scope and format of your enterprise (see Chapter 9), you can apply the creative problem solving process (with the Pugh method) to the development of a name and logo (and perhaps a slogan) for your business. A slogan example (for an insurance firm) is "You're in good hands with ALLSTATE." The goal is to have a name and slogan that are easy to remember while also giving a "picture" of what you are all about. Again, do your research to verify that the name and logo are not used and protected by other firms or enterprises. Then protect your name, logo, and slogan!

Steps in product development

So you now have a best idea, concept, or invention. Are you sufficiently motivated to move from idea to product development? Do you have the passion and discipline, as well as the ability to work with others if necessary for a successful invention (this requires both quadrant B and quadrant C thinking modes)? Are you willing to follow the seven-step development process as outlined in Table 8.4? If your business idea is a service, not a product, your "prototype" may be in the form of a small-scale pilot project, to demonstrate the feasibility of your concept and provide you with valuable customer feedback and operational information.

Table 8.4 *Steps in the Product Development Process*

1. Patent search (see Chapter 7)
2. Design work
3. **Prototype**
4. Patent application (see Chapter 7)
5. Name (logo, trademark) selection and protection
6. Packaging design and prototype refinement
7. Business plan (see Chapter 10)

Prototype

Prototype development

The prototype that is made based on the final, best solution coming out of a Pugh method evaluation is strictly for the purpose of confirming the soundness of the concept and to demonstrate it to potential purchasers. It is nearly impossible to find a licensee unless you have a working prototype. The biggest "deal killer" in business is to have a prototype that is not exactly like your proposed product. If the development process has only advanced a few rounds, prototypes may be needed to evaluate or test a number of options or alternate designs or to prove the robustness of your product. If your product involves new, unproven technology, testing may have to be quite extensive to create confidence in your product and confirm the estimated performance. The stages in prototype development are listed in Table 8.5.

Table 8.5 *Stages in Prototype Development*

1. Design stage (during the Pugh method evaluation).
2. Procurement stage (obtaining the materials and/or making the parts).
3. Assembly stage.
4. Testing stage.
5. Final industrial design stage (with full engineering drawings and specifications for production). Increasingly, this information may be in digital form to save time to market.
6. Other drawings as needed: artist's concept to sell your product and patent drawings in the specific format required by the Patent Office.

Prototype testing

Typically, all or parts of a technical design require testing to validate the decisions made. If the product will depend on new technology or application of existing technology in new ways, tests may be required to confirm the effectiveness of the technology in the design. Sometimes a test is needed to confirm estimated performance simply because the complex interplay of environmental and operating variables cannot be modeled with a computer. The construction of test models, prototypes and test apparatus can consume inordinate amounts of time (and resources). And yet, all too frequently, the tests do not provide the validation or answer the questions needed by the designers because the test was not well planned. Table 9.2 provides some guidelines for setting up a test plan.

Table 8.6 *Elements of an Effective Test Plan*

> • Statement of the specific purpose of the tests. Which decisions will the test validate or illuminate? If the test does not bear on a design decision, it most likely will not be needed.
>
> • Specific test objectives. What needs to be measured during the test, and what equipment and specifications are required?
>
> • Outline the step-by-step procedure to be used for conducting the test. If possible, use a standard protocol. What variables need to be monitored or controlled?
>
> • Outline the expected results, preferably in the form of a data sheet—if you do not know roughly what will happen, data collection and analysis are threatened. Also specify if the product is expected to be tested to destruction.

After the tests have been run, prepare a summary of the results and conclusions drawn from the testing, together with the recommendations for design changes and plans to implement the changes (if any). Make sure that no further design changes after this stage are anticipated since changes after Job 1 are very expensive and can cost you market share.

Chapter 9
Decisions on Product and Business Format

The focus of this chapter is on tasks that will primarily require the mindset of a "judge." At the conclusion of the idea evaluation process using the Pugh method, you will have obtained an in-depth understanding of the merits of your best solution or concept (be it a new product or an innovative service). So now is the time to make decisions on what to do with it. From this point on, your investment costs in your concept will go up substantially, depending on the decisions you make. We will look at the contextual thinking tasks required. It can also be very helpful to final decision making if you obtain an unbiased commercial assessment of your idea. Other decisions to be made are on the best approach of marketing your concept, either by selling the idea or patent, licensing it, or starting your own business. If you decide to start your own enterprise, you will need to decide on the most appropriate business format—franchise, individual proprietorship, partnership or corporation.

Right-brain tasks for the "judge"

Judgment is commonly perceived to be a very critical, analytical, logical, rational activity—in other words, a strictly left-brain mode. However, to do the best thinking, we must also consider some right-brain input (quadrant C, "producer" mode and quadrant D, "engineer" mode), in order to include customer aspects and the wider context of the solution, as illustrated in the "wheel" of Figure 9.1.

How strong is your personal motivation?

If the following five factors are present, you can know intuitively that your best idea is "it."

1. You really, really, really care ➤ PASSION
2. The idea just won't go away ➤ OBSESSION
3. Others care as much as you do ➤ CONTAGION
4. Making it happen is fun for you ➤ FULFILLMENT
5. The idea is much better than other alternatives ➤ SUPERIORITY

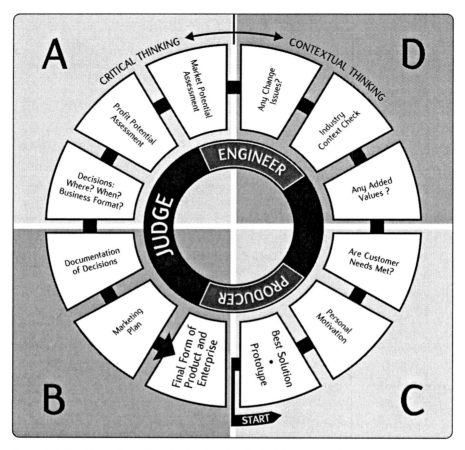

Figure 9.1 *Thinking tasks and just-in-time learning for final decisions on the product and enterprise (superimposed on the four-quadrant ABCD model developed by Ned Herrmann)*

Are all customer needs met?

You may have a personal stake and pride in your idea or invention, you may be in love with your idea, but you must not think invention—remember to THINK MARKET! Chapter 10 will present tips on how to "sell" your idea. Right now, go back to the original problem definition and make sure that all customer needs have been met.

Sometimes, novel ideas can get the problem solving process sidetracked away from the original goal—thus it is important to make this final check. If you have to decide between two or more good ideas, use the checklist in Table 9.1. In addition, if you really have two equally good, but very different ideas that cannot be combined, consider the possibility of using them both, either at the same time or in sequence.

Table 9.1 *Checklist for Final Idea Selection*

___ Can ideas be combined to obtain a higher-quality solution?

___ How well do the ideas solve the problem? Use a 7-point rating system.

___ Do the ideas meet all needs? If they pass this go/no go checkpoint, rank them according to any extra values they provide, especially if these do not increase costs.

___ Do a cost/value analysis and possibly a risk analysis on implementation.

What value can you add?

The concept of *value added* is very important if you want to have a competitive product or service. Customers often are willing to pay more if substantial added value is provided. The best scenario of course is if the added value can be included at no added cost. Be aware that value can be tangible or intangible, real or perceived.

For example, if your product happens to be at the forefront of a developing trend or fits in with the goal of a particular environmental movement, this could represent an intangible value. Aspects of being in the right place at the right time come into play here—and often this depends on luck. It helps to remember the saying, "Luck comes to those who are prepared."

Can you verify the industry context?

This angle becomes important when you prepare your business plan. You must be up-to-date and well informed about what is going on in the industry that relates to your product. Motorola missed a big opportunity for a large contract by waiting with the development of the digital phone. When AT&T was looking for a

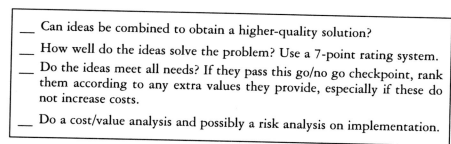

> **Frequently ask the paradigm question posed by Joel Barker:**
>
> *"What is impossible to do in my field or business today, but if it could be done, would fundamentally change what I do (or what people do)?"*
>
> Reference 1.3

supplier, Nokia, a small company in Finland, was ready and thus quickly gained a large market share. Studying trends is not just a creative thinking exercise (though valuable in itself)—it has real economic implications in the timing and success of your planned enterprise. Read trade journals; visit trade shows; search the web sites of your competitors, all while watching for trends in your product area and wider context. This cannot be overemphasized—a sudden, unanticipated paradigm shift might make your product obsolete before it is launched.

What changes will your idea or product create?

We live in a rapidly changing world. Many changes are positive, others negative. Try to anticipate the changes involved that might be associated with your product, so you can emphasize the positives and minimize the negative effects. Be aware that most people are wary of change. If priorities and values must be changed in order to innovate, intense communication will be necessary.

Left-brain tasks for the "judge"

The following tasks of definitive patent search, commercial idea assessment, and assessment of profit potential mainly require critical thinking and analytical decision making.

Assessment of market potential

A number of firms and organizations exist who are willing—for a fee—to assess the market potential of your idea. Some that were easy to access via Internet are listed in Table 9.2. Check these web sites for more information of what each service provides. You will have to use your judgment about the timing of the assessment. Some recommend that the assessment be done at the idea development stage, before any money is invested in product development, prototyping, or applying for a patent.

Table 9.2 *Sources that Can Analyze the Market Potential of an Idea*

1. Center for Entrepreneurship, Hankamer School of Business, Baylor University at **http://hsb.baylor.edu/entrepreneur**. Cost: $150.
2. WIN (World Innovation Network) Innovation Center, Southwest Missouri State University at **http://www.innovation-institute.com** Cost: $175 (U.S.), $195 elsewhere.
3. Patent Café Software available from **http://www.ipbookstore.com** (includes workbook). Cost: $69.95.

Based on the results of the commercial evaluation and information given in Chapter 7 on the patenting process, make the decision about obtaining a patent for your invention or product. Unless you have the time and ability to conduct the final, exhaustive patent search yourself, hire a competent patent attorney and initiate the patenting process. In most cases, a product that is not protected with a patent has little commercial value, either for licensing or giving your business a market advantage.

Assessment of profit potential

As soon as the figures for the costs involved in starting up and running a business have been obtained and the appropriate sales price has been decided, then it is possible to calculate the stream of profits that will be generated by the planned enterprise. These monthly projections (for two or three years) will be vital when completing the financial sheets of the business plan. They are also central to the final decision as to whether to proceed with the enterprise.

When estimating the various costs involved it is important to ensure that these are as accurate and "complete" as possible. A common fault when calculating startup and operating costs is to omit or undervalue the entrepreneur's own time. This must be included on a realistic basis in order to make the correct decision as to whether the enterprise is sensible or not. A simple way to value your input is to calculate what you could earn at an hourly rate if you spent the time working on another project or as an employee. The weekly or monthly value is simply this rate multiplied by the (often very high) number of hours that you will work.

The market research and comparisons with competing alternatives analyzed during the Pugh Method evaluation will give a good indication of the price that will attract the levels of demand that have been assumed in the calculation of operating costs. Monthly revenues are simply calculated by multiplying this price by the expected level of sales. In many cases there is a considerable time lag—certainly weeks, and sometimes months—between selling (invoicing) and payment. Typical payment terms of key market customers should be ascertained and built into the monthly projection of revenues. This delay or "trade credit" may also be available to the entrepreneur, although it is often the case that new businesses with little or no track record will be required to pay suppliers in advance until their creditworthiness is proven through experience.

The extent to which delayed payment by customers and advance payment to suppliers places pressure upon the cash flow of the business can vary significantly. Many retailers can often benefit from immediate payment by customers and one month's trade credit from suppliers. Also, these pressures may impact service providers less strongly whereas manufacturing firms may be affected greatly.

The decision to proceed can be viewed as a decision to invest in the enterprise. When making an investment, one of the main aims is to maximize the returns that will be generated. In short, the decision to proceed is only sensible if there are no alternative investment possibilities that would provide a higher return for the same level of commitment. At its simplest, this could just refer to the rate of interest that would be realized if the equivalent level of funding were invested in a savings account at the prevailing rate of interest.

Given the expected revenues and costs that have been estimated for the first two or three years of the business, it is possible to compare the profit stream (revenues minus costs) with the investment income that would be generated if the startup investment earned interest in a savings account. This relatively straightforward calculation refers to the **net present value** (NPV) of future profits generated by the business (also known as **discounting**). A formula for this calculation is given in Table 9.3 (with an alternate step-by-step format offered in Table 9.4 for the less mathematically minded). Since it is not unusual for an innovative company to run at a loss for a number of years before the idea "takes off," it may be necessary to run your profit projections beyond the near term. Also, during the startup years, entrepreneurs cannot always expect to be paid a salary equivalent to what they might be paid as an employee in a comparable position elsewhere. Entrepreneurs are advised to keep their current jobs until their projections show that the new enterprise can support them at least at a level of 60 percent of previous salary before they resign and work full time in their new business. This is a difficult call to make because of the risks as well as the intangible benefits involved.

Table 9.3 _Formula for Calculating the Future Value of Money_

A simple formula can be used to calculate the future value of money.

$$\$_{Future} = \$_{Present}(1+i)^n$$

where n is the number of years and i is the interest rate.

For example $100 for two years at an interest rate of 10% is

$$\$_{Future} = 100(1+0.1)(1+0.1) = \$121.$$

For discounting, we simply find the present value of future money, or

$$\$_{Present} = \$_{Future}/(1+i)^n$$

Thus, $121 two years hence at 10% would have a present value of

$$\$_{Present} = 121/[(1+0.1)(1+0.1)] = \$100$$

Table 9.4 *Calculation of Net Present Value*

Most people understand the process of discounting much more easily when it operates in the opposite direction. If asked the value of $100 in a year's time at 10% interest, most will crack straight back with the correct answer of $110. If you left it gaining interest for a additional year, it would grow to $121 ($110 + 10% of $110). Discounting is simply the same process in reverse. $110 in one year's time with an interest rate at 10% has a present value of $100. $121 in two year's time with a prevailing interest rate of 10% also has a present value of $100.

To calculate the present value of the profit stream expected from your business over future years, simply follow the steps below:

• The present value of the profits (or losses) made after one year is arrived at by dividing these by the rate of interest. For example, if the rate were 10%, you would divide by 1.1, if 5% by 1.05, if 20% by 1.2. In the example above, this would mean dividing $110 by 1.1, giving a present value of $100.

• To find the present value of the second year's profits (or losses) simply divide in the same way, but apply the interest twice. If the interest rate were 10%, this would be 1.1 x 1.1 = 1.21, if it were 5%, it would be 1.05 x 1.05 = 1.1025, and if the interest rate is 20%, then this would be 1.2 x 1.2 = 1.44.

• In the case of the third year, use exactly the same calculation but simply multiply the interest rate three times rather that twice to arrive at the figure by which you divide the profit (loss).

• Continue this process of multiplying for each additional year the interest rate for a further time until you reach the end of your projected profit stream.

• Sum the numbers calculated for each year and subtract this from the startup costs of the business.

• If the resulting figure, the Net Present Value, is higher than your startup costs, your business expects to generate a higher return than would result from investing the startup costs in a savings account at a prevailing rate of interest. If it is lower, then proceed no further!!

The Say quote (from 200 years ago but still valid) emphasizes the importance of allowing for the unexpected in your calculations. Sales may not go as expected, and payment delays may be longer than your market research indicated. Similarly, costs may be higher than anticipated, or suppliers may let you down in terms of quality or promptness of delivery or both. It

> *In the course of such complex operations, there is an abundance of obstacles to be surmounted, anxieties to be repressed, misfortunes to be repaired and expedients to be devised.*
>
> Jean Baptiste Say

is sensible therefore to recalculate the net present value with more pessimistic assumptions about revenues and costs in order to ascertain how sensitive the business fortunes are to changing market conditions. To cheer yourself up, you might also wish to recalculate on the basis of more optimistic assumptions so long as you treat these as "hoped for" rather than actual. They may turn out to be realistic, but don't bank on it!

You may be surprised to observe how much higher than the cost of production the price of your product or service has to be to ensure an acceptable return on your investment. As mentioned in Chapter 8, a rule of thumb for a manufactured product's selling price states that the price will need to be three to five times the production costs in order to realize a sufficient level of profit to justify the investment. In the case of services and retail trade, this ratio may be lower, but should still be more than 2:1. The reason for this will be clear if you have properly calculated the full costs of taking your concept to market. In addition to the hidden labor costs that you and others may contribute, many other large commitments are involved with marketing and making the target consumers aware of your product or service and the related benefits.

TIPS: (a) If the return from your business is only slightly higher than prevailing interest rates, then you should consult current financial publications to determine whether there is a consensus as to the future direction that interest rates might take. If they are anticipated to rise significantly, your investment could cost you dearly! (b) If you found the calculations of cost and profit potential difficult, we recommend that you either take a course in business accounting or at the least acquire a trustworthy partner with accounting skills.

Business decisions

You may be well suited to entrepreneurship and well qualified to establish the enterprise of your choice, but you may be unaware as to where to locate and when to start.

Where should you locate?

Location is critical both in terms of the market being targeted and the costs that will confront the business. Choice of location may be one of the first tests of the entrepreneur's quality of judgment and decision making. Take the time and effort necessary to select the location of your business. Who are your potential customers and where are they located? Will you be "visible" as well as easily accessible by drive-by or walk-by potential customers? If applicable, will you have convenient parking? Also, who will be your suppliers and where are they located? If you are dealing with perishable raw materials, this is not a trivial consideration. Who are your competitors and where are they located? Will you be able to find qualified employees when you are ready to expand? For example, one automotive design supplier chose a location 500 miles from Detroit (the home of the "big three" automakers) because of the extremely tough competition for skilled designers there. The new location, which has a technical university nearby, is a ready source of skilled designers at much more reasonable cost.

If you do not want to or cannot change your location, you can use creative thinking to identify a market niche or consumer need in your present location. Many startups begin in the entrepreneur's home or garage. In the US, the SBA estimates that as many as 20 percent of new small businesses are operated from the owner's home. With many new computer-based businesses, this number is growing. Contact the local Chamber of Commerce for information about locating your business in a particular location.

When should you start your business?

Market conditions are often volatile both in terms of demand for products or services and in terms of the technological changes that are occurring. The timing of the launch may be critical in sustaining the business through the early and often most vulnerable stage of its development. Rushing to bring a product to market before its technical bugs have been worked out or producing a 2003 product for the 2004 market are equally detrimental for the success of your enterprise.

If you have done a thorough job in going through the creative problem solving steps, completed your business plan and worked out your cash flow for one to three years, you will almost be ready to launch your business. You may want to do a last check with a trusted friend or expert who has had experience with launching a business, and also keep your eyes wide-open to economic conditions and trends, as well as unexpected surprises. Learn as much as you can based on current information, then make your decision.

Choosing a business format

Basically, you have two choices of what to do with your invention:

1. You can sell the patent outright or license someone to manufacture and market the product.

2. You can go into business yourself.

Licensing

History shows that many inventions/patents were sold to companies for relatively small fees, with the companies later making huge profits from a successful product. Today, the trend is more toward licensing products that have a good market potential and fit in with a company's business.

The advantages of licensing are that you keep ownership of your product, yet you have low overhead, no need to hire employees, few administrative responsibilities, no cash flow worries, and no buying, selling, and bill collecting. Your licensor will market your product, keep inventory, and take care of distribution. Depending on the product, the licensor may also be involved in manufacturing or assembly (or farm these tasks out). Since the licensor will have existing infrastructure, there is a substantial time saving in getting the product to market.

The main disadvantage of licensing is that you lose control of your product. You will be tied to the fortunes of the licensor, and the deal may not bring in large revenues. Charles Stanley, Vice President at Motorola, lists some key items you need to watch if you want to sell an invention to a large company (see Table 9.5).

Table 9.5 *Selling Your Idea or Invention to a Large Company*

1. Your intellectual property must be protected. Companies are leery of accusations of cheating, especially if the company is working on a similar idea.
2. Don't consider companies as venture capitalists.
3. Your idea must be closely related to the company's core business.
4. Do your homework! Be sure your idea is not obsolete, wrong or economically nonviable.
5. Be realistic in your royalty expectations.
6. Have an "elevator" speech ready (see Chapter 10).
7. Use the web and go to conferences on topics related to your idea to identify potential company champions.

The good news is that most large companies buy more ideas and technology from outside than they develop internally. If you want to exploit this opportunity, you will need to develop good "selling" skills (as will be explained in Chapter 10).

Starting your own business

If you decide that you want to be an entrepreneur and run your own business, you have several options in how to get started and for the legal form your business can take.

1. You can buy an existing business—either one that is thriving or one that is in bankruptcy. Depending on your business idea, this may be an ideal fit, and you may acquire the infrastructure, a good location, and a customer list, saving you much time and trouble. The key is to make sure that you have a good fit.

2. You can buy a franchise, as discussed on the following page.

3. You can buy someone else's business idea, patent or invention through a patent broker or from InventNet or a not-for-profit R&D institution or university, but then you will still need to decide on the legal form of your business.

Legal forms for startup businesses

If you must have complete control and be the person solely responsible, the sole proprietorship is for you. But make sure that your own qualifications and competencies are sufficient to start and run your own business.

Or could you profit by including others with complementary skills? If you decide that you need a partner or team, good judgment will be required to set up the best ownership structure, controls and incentives. These need to be established at the outset and will have a strong influence on the future success of the business. If you need some expert help in some aspects of running your business (including financing) and if you have already worked with a co-inventor or co-developer (or a close friend or family member), then a partnership might be the ideal setup. A strong team can make the difference between success and a marginal/failed venture or between a so-so and a great company.

A small Subchapter-S corporate structure with a small group of shareholders closely holding their shares and substantially participating in running the business may be an alternative with attractive tax advantages. We recommend that you research your options carefully and consult an attorney to set up the legal structure of your business. Make sure you obtain all necessary local and State licenses and registrations.

Franchising

This provides easy access to an established product, thus reducing the many risks of a new business. However, franchising requires all the self-analysis of starting a small business. Best get legal help when you get to the step of examining the franchiser's contract.

The advantages of franchising include:

- Significantly better success rate than a new business.
- Reduced risk and less operating capital.
- Marketing plan and promotional materials in place.
- Quality control standards established.
- Available technical and management assistance (including training).
- Opportunities for growth through the right to sub-franchise.
- Opportunity to gain experience in running a business.

The disadvantages of franchising are:

- Service cost.
- Restrictions on freedom of ownership.
- Limited expansion.
- Termination of agreement.
- Low performance of other franchisees can influence your business.

Simple Example: Taxi Driver as a Franchise

A major city in Canada has only one taxi company. If you want a franchise, you are assigned a taxi for which you are required to pay a fixed amount per month. The franchiser provides maintenance of the taxi, dispatcher services, and company name, the franchisee the gasoline and oil. Minimum contract agreement is for one year. In the agreement, franchisees are not allowed to start a competing company for at least one year after the termination of the franchise contract. Because of the increase in business, two new taxi companies are now starting to compete with the existing monopoly. This begins to seriously cut into the business of the existing taxi company. Some drivers signed the original contract with the knowledge that business would increase because of increasing population and industrial growth. Now they see a decline rather than an increase in their revenue and opportunities.

Moral of this example: Look carefully before you leap into a franchise!

Decision-making documentation

Why is it important to keep good records of your entire problem-solving and decision making process? The rationales for making decisions are frequently omitted from many project reports and design documents. If you have done a good job in making decisions and have selected the best alternative after a thorough analysis of all the options against the objectives (or Pugh method criteria), the rationale is simply a summary of the results of this process. Omitting this information might invite needless questioning about the decision later and perhaps repetition of the selection evaluation process.

Cases of "re-inventing the wheel" can sometimes be traced to a lack of information on why a particular choice was made upstream in the process. When competing alternatives are closely matched, there may be a tendency to omit rationales for decisions to avoid undermining confidence in the decision. This would be a mistake, since the recipient of the design would lose valuable information that may allow or dissuade a design change later on. More often than not, the designer or inventor may gain confidence and favor by bending over backward to describe the competing alternatives at least as well as the one selected. All designs and inventions must be sold to someone; most must be sold many times. It is simply not enough to present a drawing or a prototype. A concise and easy-to-follow summary of the evolution of the product which includes the decision rationale is essential. (Ref. 3.5).

Also, having a good record of your invention's development (in the prescribed format) is essential to substantiate your claim as the original inventor. In addition, a complete case file on the development of your product, including all information on the context, will be invaluable when you compile your business plan (in Chapter 10).

And last but not least, a complete documentation of your business startup (including both the successes as well as those things that did not work out as predicted) will become a valuable database for continuing improvement or starting another enterprise.

Developing a marketing plan

You can profitably use the creative problem solving process to develop your marketing approach. If you are marketing an innovative product or invention that has no previous track record for marketing and sales, you may want to conduct some marketing tests or trials using prototypes or trial runs of your final product. As you have seen with the example of the Post-it notes (in Chapter 5), you may have to come up with a creative marketing approach if the first trials fail but you are still convinced you have a great product.

Guidelines for developing a marketing plan are available at the website **www.sba.gov/starting/indexbusplans.html** as part of their materials available on business planning. As you carefully work through the three sections of the guidelines, you will gain a basic understanding of your market and your marketing strategies.

The deep understanding about your idea that you have gained from conducting a thorough evaluation and obtaining a "best" concept will be crucial as you develop your marketing plan. Whether your business will be based on offering a product or a service, you may have realized by now that it will likely involve both to some degree. If you will sell a product, its competitiveness will surely be tied to the service that you intend to provide; if you offer a service, its satisfactory execution will often depend on the products or tools you will use or furnish as part of your service.

Marketing involves several key components, as listed in Table 9.6 (based on information in Ref. 9.2).

Table 9.6 *Key Elements of Marketing*

1. Market research — for understanding your customers, competition, and trends.
2. Advertising — to get your message to potential customers.
3. Sales — the outcome of marketing, with a satisfied customer and a fair price for your product.
4. Public relations — tell the story of your successful enterprise to create a favorable image.
5. Strategies — database marketing (from a purchased database) or direct marketing.
6. Product promotion — here you can be especially creative to quickly (and memorably) get your product into the marketplace.
7. Pricing — a crucial, though often neglected part of marketing; make sure you focus on value, not on lowest price to be competitive.
8. Distribution — how will you get your product to the customer? You may want to use more than one approach to meet your customer's needs.

The marketing plan will become an important component of the overall business plan (described in Chapter 10) and requires very detailed information and research about the customers and market niche you are targeting, as well as about your competitors. Typical questions to be investigated have been arranged into three categories and are given in Table 9.7 (for product/service analysis, Table 9.8 (for market analysis), and Table 9.9 (for marketing strategies/marketing mix).

Table 9.7 *Product/Service Analysis Questions (from SBA)*

1. Describe your product and what it does.
2. What advantages does your product/service have over those of your competition (consider unique features, patents, expertise, special training, etc.)?
3. What disadvantages does it have?
4. Where and how will you get your materials and supplies?
5. Where and how will you get qualified employees?

Table 9.8 *A Sample of SBA Questions for Market Analysis*

1. Who are your customers—private sector, wholesalers, retailers, government, other? What is the percent distribution for each?
2. What is the target industry? What is the target geographic area?
3. What product lines and sales will you target?
4. How much will the selected market spend on your type of product this year?
5. Who are your competitors? List each main competitor by name, how long in business, the market share, the price and strategy, and the distinct product/service features.
6. List your strengths and weaknesses compared to your competitors (consider location, size of resources, reputation, services, as well as personnel).
7. Look at the following economic factors that will affect your product or service: country growth, industry health, economic trends, taxes, rising energy prices.
8. What legal and government factors could affect your market? What are other environmental factors that could affect you, but over which you have no control?

Table 9.9 *A Sample of SBA Questions for Marketing Strategies*

1. What kind of image do you want to have (such as cheap but good, or customer-oriented, or exclusiveness, or higher quality, or convenience, or speed, or extra value, or innovative, or...)?

2. What features will you emphasize?

3. What is your pricing strategy (markup on cost; suggested price; competitive; below competition; premium price; other)? Are your prices in line with your image? Do your prices cover costs (sales, warranty, training, product development) and a margin of profit?

4. What customer services will you provide? What are terms for sales/credit? What services does the competition offer?

5. What things do you wish to say about your business (write a 40-word paragraph)?

6. What promotional sources will you use (television, radio, direct mail, personal contacts, trade associations, newspapers, magazines, yellow pages, billboard, website, product demos or give-away, other)? Why do you think the media you have chosen are the most effective? Will you use an innovative approach?

MARKETING TIPS FOR ENTREPRENEURS

The customer is always right — at least almost always!

Customer expectations change — be alert for quick response!

Learn from your competitors — do not underestimate them!

Do not overestimate your product (or service) — be realistic!

Your employees project your company's image — train them!

Resources

9.1 Jeffry A. Timmons, *New Venture Creation: Entrepreneurship for the 21st Century*, 5th edition, IRWIN/McGraw-Hill, 1999.

9.2 Jack Ferreri, *Successful Sales and Marketing: Smart Ways to Boost Your Bottom Line*, Guide #1809, Book 4 of Entrepreneur Magazine's Business Management Series, Entrepreneur Media, Inc., Irvine, California, 1999; see www.smallbizbooks.com.

Chapter 10
Starting Your Creative Enterprise

In this concluding chapter, we want to show you how to use the producer's mindset to do some of the tasks needed for actually starting a new business, as outlined in Figure 10.1. Launching an enterprise (or implementing a solution) is in itself a new problem, which requires a new round of creative problem solving or whole-brain thinking with emphasis on the producer's mindset. If you want to license your idea, you have to "sell" the idea to an appropriate company—with a brief message. If you have decided that you want to build a business on your idea, you need to know where to find financing for your enterprise.

Other practical topics touched on are long-range strategies for remaining competitive and how to "keep on moving" beyond startup. Many of the Part 2 tasks now feed into writing your business plan. Also, you will review the creative problem-solving process as you survey how to avoid common mistakes to succeed in your business. Finally, you will complete a pre-launch checklist and an assessment of what you have learned.

"Selling" your idea—with an elevator speech

When contacting a company with the purpose of selling your invention, talk business opportunity, not just invention. Establish your credibility and be business-like. Most companies think of inventors as someone from Planet Pluto.

> ### Sell yourself.
> ### Sell your invention.
> ### Sell the business opportunity.

The person to contact in a company will usually have a title such as *New Product Development Manager* or *Director of Marketing* or *Director of Research and Development*. He or she will usually not discuss your idea if it is not ready for the marketplace. It is therefore essential to have a working prototype and patent protection if appropriate. You must also be prepared to give an effective, concise opening presentation—a so-called "elevator speech" or 30-second message.

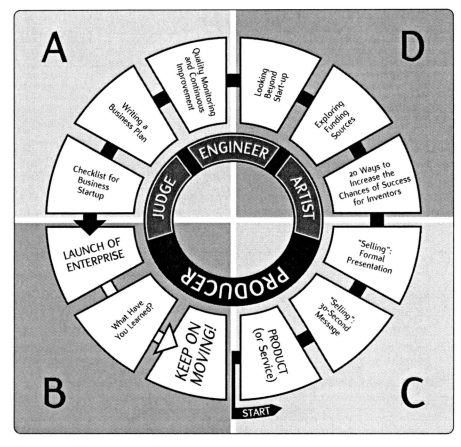

Figure 10.1 *Thinking tasks and just-in-time information for obtaining funding, launching your enterprise and evaluating your learning (superimposed on the four-quadrant ABCD model developed by Ned Herrmann)*

Why only 30 seconds?

Milo O. Frank, a business communications consultant, has written a poignant book on *How to Get Your Point Across in 30 Seconds—or Less* (Simon and Schuster, 1986). This approach is especially helpful when you want a specific response from people—when you are asking them to do something for you.

In our busy times, when our message has to compete with a bombardment of messages and information "noise" from many different directions and sources (just think of e-mail), how can we make sure that we are being heard? Some reasons for being brief are listed in Table 10.1. For impact, "short" is usually better than "long."

Table 10.1 *Why Messages Should Be Brief*

> - Memos and letters of request are too long and thus frequently get tossed out unread.
> - The attention span of the average person is 30 seconds.
> - Doctors listen to their patients for an average of only 19 seconds before they start making a diagnosis and proceed with the physical exam (according to research done at Michigan State University).
> - Time has become compressed; communication is now often by email or answering machine message.
> - TV commercials do a good job of getting their message across in 30 seconds.
> - In the US, TV news sound bites typically are 30 seconds long or they do not get airtime.
> - Most importantly, if you can't say it in 30 seconds, you probably are not thinking about your message clearly. You may need more time to present supplementary information (if asked), but the main thrust of your message should be very concise.
> - President Abraham Lincoln's Gettysburg address is a brief but very powerful message. It is discussed at the end of this section.

Preparation

People often think that preparing such a brief message would be a breeze. However, it takes much thinking (using the creative problem solving process) and can easily take an hour or more, especially for beginners. The messages can be verbal or written: telephone requests and messages left with staff members; memos, letters, e-mail, thank-you notes, faxes; abstracts for proposals and scholarly papers, formal presentations at meetings, interviews, sales solicitations or complaints; social situations with superiors, chance meetings, and giving toasts. The brief time in an elevator may be all the time you have to present your creative idea to a company's president. And an important application for entrepreneurs is attracting the interest of a venture capitalist or business angel.

As you prepare your message, you must determine your objective, your audience, and your strategy.

Objective: What do you want to achieve? Why? You need a clear-cut, single, specific objective.

Audience: Who can get you what you want? Know what your audience is going to want from you. Make sure you go to the right person or the right group— those who will make the decisions you need.

Approach: How can you get what you want? Brainstorm different ideas, then select the one that meets the objective and audience best, in form as well as content. Ask yourself: What is the basis of my game plan? What is the heart of my message? What is the single best statement that will lead to what I want? How will this statement relate to the needs of the audience? What is my sales pitch?

Message

Next comes work on the three parts of the message: hook, subject, and close.

Hook: To get attention, the hook is often in the form of a question. You may use humor (at your own expense only) or a visual aid. The hook is a bridge connecting the audience to what you want. In a very brief message, the entire message can be the hook. You can use the Herrmann model in Table 10.2 to ensure you communicate with your audience in all four thinking quadrants.

Table 10.2 *Effective Communications Checklist (©1998 The Ned Herrmann Group)*

Quadrant A – Clarity
___ Do you have concise facts?
___ Are you providing quantitative data?
___ Will the audience have the same understanding of your words as you do?
___ Are the arguments or analysis supporting your position logical?

Quadrant B – Action Plan
___ Does your request ask for well-planned, orderly implementation?
___ Are you providing the necessary details?
___ Is your message well-organized, neat, and in an appropriate format?
___ Do you know when to stop?

Quadrant C – Emotional Appeal
___ Are you reaching the heart of the audience by sharing emotions?
___ Are you relating personal failures, experiences, and examples?
___ Are you user-friendly and building relationships?

Quadrant D – Imagery
___ Are you painting a memorable creative word picture or metaphor.
___ Are you using a colorful, imaginative visual aid?
___ Are you providing context, a look at the future, the "big picture"?
___ Are the concepts sound or clear?
___ Are you addressing the problem of change?

Subject: Answer who, what, where, when, why, and how as they relate directly to your explicit or hidden objective. Does the message correspond with your approach? Is it made relevant to your audience? What are the benefits to the audience?

Close: This is the bottom line. A message without a close is a wasted opportunity. Be forceful or subtle in asking for what you want, depending on your audience. Demand a specific action within a stated time frame, or ask for a reaction through the power of suggestion.

Oral Presentation

In an oral presentation, appearance, "acting," and mode of speaking are important since they help transmit the meaning of the message.

Style and appearance: Monitor your body language. Practice delivering your message in front of friends who can critique you in a supportive way. Or have your practice presentation videotaped and then critically evaluate your performance. Examine your facial expressions, eye contact, posture, gestures, and tone of voice. Check your appearance—do you know what types of clothes make you look your best? Are you aware that some features in your appearance (for example body piercing or dreadlocks) may give a negative impression? Consideration of others takes precedence over your own tastes.

Acting: Transmit a positive attitude. Smile. Focus on different people in the audience while you speak. Do not read off a script or memorize your speech. You may feel that you are being asked to pretend. To some degree, that is what good communicators do. A prime example is former US President Ronald Reagan.

Mode of speaking: Do not use offensive words! Instead, show surprise, puzzlement, or concern in your facial expression and voice as you speak. Learn to modulate your voice (avoid a monotone); use strategic pauses. Practice breathing and relaxation techniques prior to the start to reduce your stress level and thus have your voice sound more natural.

Written Messages

Write legibly and neatly. Use good grammar and correct spelling. Be positive and friendly. Do not detract from your message by an overuse of fancy fonts, color and clip art—a little bit can go a long way but only if it supports your message.

ABRAHAM LINCOLN'S GETTYSBURG ADDRESS

Four score and seven years ago, our fathers brought forth upon this continent a new nation: conceived in liberty, and dedicated to the proposition that "all men are created equal."

Now we are engaged in a great civil war, testing whether that nation, or any nation so conceived and so dedicated, can long endure. We are met on a great battlefield of that war. We have come to dedicate a portion of it as a final resting place for those who here gave their lives that the nation might live. It is altogether fitting and proper that we should do this. But, in a larger sense, we cannot dedicate – we cannot consecrate – we cannot hallow this ground. The brave men, living and dead, who struggled here, have consecrated it, far above our poor power to add or detract. The world will little note, nor long remember, what we say here, but it can never forget what they did here.

It is for us, the living, rather to be dedicated here to the unfinished work which they who fought here have, thus far, so nobly carried on. It is rather for us to be here dedicated to the great task remaining before us – that from these honored dead we take increased devotion to that cause for which they gave the last full measure of devotion – that we here highly resolve that these dead shall not have died in vain; that this nation, under God, shall have a new birth of freedom, and that government of the people, by the people, for the people, shall not perish from the earth.

The Setting

The battle of Gettysburg (in Pennsylvania) was fought on July 1-3, 1863. More than 7000 soldiers from the Union North and the Confederate South died there, and a national soldiers cemetery was created to properly inter more than 3500 Union casualties lying in hasty, inadequate graves all over the battlefield. (The Confederate remains were moved to cemeteries in the South after the end of the war.) The dedication of the national cemetery was held on November 19, 1863, less than halfway through the reburial process. Edward Everett (former governor of Massachusetts, President of Harvard University, US Secretary of State, and noted orator) gave the opening speech. Next came Union President Abraham Lincoln. There was little reaction, and many of those present did not even realize he had been speaking.

Aftermath

The following day, Everett wrote to Lincoln (who had thought his speech a failure), *"I should be glad if I could flatter myself that I came as near to the central idea of the occasion in two hours as you did in two minutes."*

According to www.gettysburg.com/bog/ga.htm, the 272 words of the Gettysburg Address were formulated with great thought by Lincoln. He wrote the first draft in Washington shortly before November 18 and revised it at the home of David Wills in Gettysburg the night before the dedication. "The speech transformed Gettysburg from a scene of carnage into a symbol, giving meaning to the sacrifice of the dead and inspiration to the living."

The short Gettysburg address came to be one of the most important documents in the growth of American democracy, according to http://usinfo.state.gov/usa/infousa/facts/democrac/25.htm, because it asserted the true meaning of the constitution, that all men really were created equal, slaves included. Also, before this speech, the United States were spoken of in the plural; after the speech, the United States truly became a union seen in the singular ("the United States is…").

Analysis

Objective: To state the grand purpose of the war, "a union, with liberty and freedom for all," while giving meaning to the sacrifice made by the soldiers.

Audience: Attendees at the dedication of the battlefield cemetery, but with the press attending, the nation, and the world (posterity) were also included.

Approach: A concise statement in 10 sentences.

Hook: First three sentences, forming a bridge connecting the past vision to the present experience of the audience.

Message: Five sentences, dedicating the cemetery and honoring the sacrifice and bravery of the soldiers, living and dead.

Close: Two sentences, calling for the living to dedicate themselves to the work that the nation, under God, will be a government of the people, for the people, by the people.

Thinking quadrants addressed:

A: Facts and time span mentioned in the "hook" (sentences 1, 2, 3).

B: "Proper" dedication (sentences 4, 5).

C: Personal commitment demanded and emotion expressed (close).

D: Grand concept of "one nation, under God, with freedom for all."

Selling your idea—formal team presentation

This looks like an appropriate time to present some tips on how to make an effective team project presentation (from 15 to 30 minutes in length). The credibility of your problem-solving project may hinge on how effectively you can present your solution. Even experienced teams can benefit from rehearsing their presentation—but it is essential for people who are not used to public speaking. Another purpose for a rehearsal is to ensure that all your audio-visual equipment is working flawlessly, and that you or one of the team members know how to operate the equipment—there is nothing more frustrating for an audience than watching a team fumbling around and wasting time.

Your main objective may be to inform your audience about your project and accomplishments. But keep a secondary objective in mind also—to give a presentation that will make it easy for your audience to remember your message. Some tips to accomplish this are listed in Table 10.3.

Table 10.3 *Tips for Making an Effective Presentation*

- Start and finish on time!!!
- Make sure each person on your team is introduced clearly.
- Speak the language of your audience and state the purpose of your presentation.
- Use visualization to aid in remembering your main ideas.
- Plan time for questions at the end; respond directly to the questions.
- Be yourself; project energy, enthusiasm, and competence. Don't exaggerate or criticize.
- Typical listeners can only remember three to five points, and then only if the points are reinforced. Thus you must
  - Preview the main points to have the listeners anticipate them.
  - Continuously tie the points to the structure of the presentation.
  - Provide summaries as handouts if you have many details.
  - At the end, reiterate the main points to provide closure.

You can also use these tips for making effective solo presentations. There are many opportunities for presentations when starting a business, but none is more critical than when asking for funding. Together with submitting a written business plan, you may well be required to make a presentation to the decision makers (bank, venture capitalists, or business angels).

Twenty ways to increase the chances of success (for inventors)

The following discussion constitutes a quick review of applications for the creative problem solving mindsets and offers tips on how to avoid some common mistakes inventors make when starting an enterprise. Note that half of them occur during the implementation phase.

Inventions usually fail for one of two broad reasons:
• Development of the idea reveals serious technical problems.
• The inventor makes mistakes.

In terms of sheer numbers, "inventor mistakes" win by a mile. The good news is that most of these failures are easily avoided by periodically going through the following checklist to make sure you have paid attention to these important items. The items have been grouped according to the steps in the creative problem solving process and were adapted from information given at **www.nesta.org.uk/topic/success.html**.

Problem definition ("explorer" and "detective")

1. Do a proper patent and product search to make sure your idea is original. In most cases, unoriginal means unprotectable and consequently potentially worthless commercially.

2. Research the market properly and interpret the findings realistically. Make sure that you are developing an idea that meets a demonstrated need. Do not skip the customer surveys and analysis.

3. Conduct a complete problem analysis. Is your solution addressing the real problem? Also, have you considered simplicity and reasonable costs? Have you minimized expected change in user behavior?

4. Make sure your knowledge and skills are up-to-date and that you are familiar with the latest developments and trends.

Idea generation, evaluation and optimization ("artist," "engineer," and "judge")

5. Focus on progress and continuous improvement of your product or process. This is more important than merely having a good patent.

6. Make use of confidentiality agreements; this way, others can help in the developing process without affecting disclosure and patentability of your idea.

7. Use your available resources wisely. Going into debt can take your creative energy and focus away from developing your idea.

8. Iron out basic technical flaws before presenting your idea. Using such evaluation techniques as the Pugh method will help you identify and overcome flaws and bring out the strengths of your idea.

9. Consider working with experts; they may offer specialized knowledge that can help you and views you may have overlooked. Or consider working with a mentally diverse team to gain different viewpoints.

10. Listen to good advice but beware of flatterers.

Solution implementation and "selling" your idea ("producer")

11. Carefully evaluate your associates and commercial firms you are hiring to assist you in the patenting or licensing process.

12. Investigate opportunities in small companies, not just the market leaders, when seeking a royalty deal.

13. Make sure you have a complete idea or product with a working prototype before you make your presentation.

14. Is business your true motive? Recognize that the ideas of others can make your idea work better (even if this may hurt your ego).

15. Use all your skills and careful preparation to make an effective presentation when "selling" your ideas to a company. Remember that your "customer" or audience is interested in the business opportunity, not the invention.

16. Have realistic expectations about the worth of your idea when negotiating with a company or investor.

17. Learn from good negotiating agreements; learn to recognize decent deals.

18. In a royalty deal, be aware that at some stage it is necessary to "let go" and give up control of your idea.

19. Have a Plan B (or even a Plan C) in case your Plan A for selling your idea fails. This prevents you from selling your idea for peanuts.

20. Recognize that the action of some inventors have created an adverse image for inventors. Thus make sure your idea or product is presented in a business-like, logical fashion, so it (and you) will be taken seriously.

TIP: Although this list was specifically prepared for inventors, if you substitute "idea" or "concept" or "solution" for "invention you can see that it is useful for all entrepreneurs who want to be effective problem solvers.

Exploring startup funding for entrepreneurs

A study published in 1999 by University of Warwick economics professor Andrew Oswald found that seed money was the key factor in enabling people to run their own businesses. This was particularly true for people in their early twenties. Although a surprisingly large number of people in industrialized countries would like to be self-employed, the lack of capital is seen as the biggest hindrance, and funding is the area where entrepreneurs need help the most.

Access to finance for entrepreneurial activity varies significantly according to the nature and scale of the enterprise. Figure 10.2 shows a diagram of the different funding paths.

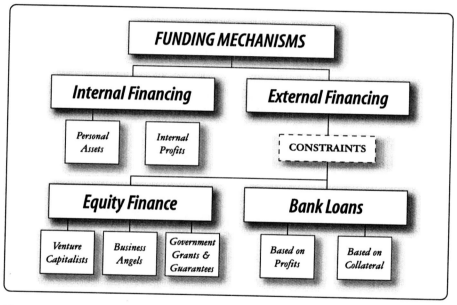

Figure 10.2 *Sources of financing for enterprise startup*

Internal financing

Many highly successful enterprises started trading at a modest level of activity. The financial requirements for startup were similarly modest and within the capabilities of the entrepreneurs, their partners, and their companies. *Organic growth* then provided sufficient profits for the enterprise to be self-financed. Short-term bank debt may be used to accommodate fluctuations in working capital (for example to compensate for seasonal cycles in the business or bridge predictable cash-flow problems), or the customers may be willing to pay up front with their orders.

To help organic growth, startup entrepreneurs initially may take very little compensation from the business—profits are used to grow the company. Or they support the business with income from another job. A BostonBank study showed that the two most important funding sources by far for MIT-related startups were the founder's *personal assets* and company cash flow (as shown in Fig. 10.3). Between 1990 and 2000, MIT graduates started over 2000 companies—of these, only about 100 were built on MIT licenses and patents (Source: http://web.mit.edu/newsoffice/founders).

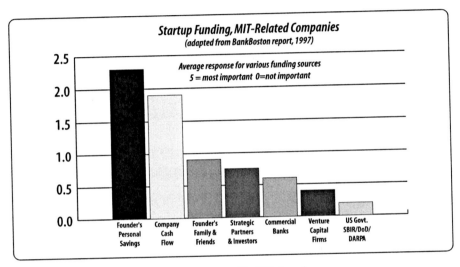

Figure 10.3 Funding sources for companies started by MIT alumni

Financing from external sources

For many businesses the prospect of self-sufficient organic growth is not an option, for several reasons:

- The lead-time from prototype to delivery may be too long to be accommodated through internal sources.
- The minimum scale of operation for competitive startup may be too large.
- The required growth rate for effective market penetration may be too rapid.
- Or the entrepreneur has only very limited personal assets or internal access to funds.

In all these cases, it will be necessary to access external financial support. It should be emphasized, however, that in the case where the only barrier is lack of personal resources, it might still be possible to pursue the organic growth option on the basis of a small injection of external funds to get started.

Constraints involved in external finance

Access to external funding for entrepreneurial activity is constrained by the risk assessment made when an external provider is involved. Judgments about the use of internally generated funds are the responsibility of the entrepreneur and are made on the basis of the information available and the risk that is tolerated. The involvement of a third party introduces new elements to both the available information and the level of risk aversion. For the entrepreneur, the key issues are access to finance on agreeable terms. For the external provider, the key issues are risk and return. To assess these accurately may require significant amounts of information about the entrepreneur, the business and the market. Getting this information costs money.

The potential provider of external finance will have two key concerns when attempting to assess risk and return. The first is to avoid choosing badly and funding an enterprise that turns out to be far more risky than anticipated. The second is to ensure that the entrepreneur will stick to his or her side of the bargain and live up to the agreements made. To determine the level of risk involved requires a significant investment in evaluation costs. To ensure that the business is run well may require significant monitoring activities. These natural constraints confronting entrepreneurs and potential providers of external finance are reflected in different ways according to the particular source of external support that is pursued.

Equity finance

Potential providers of external equity are risking their money to buy a stake in your business. Their main motive is capital gain resulting from a rapid increase in the value of the business. They are risking their capital in the sense that if the business fails, they will lose part or all of their investment. Since they are investing in the prospects of your business, they must be prepared to invest in the evaluation and possibly, later, the monitoring processes required for effective risk and return assessment.

1. **Venture capitalists**—Institutional providers of external equity finance use their past and present experience of deal making as a guide to the potential costs of evaluation and monitoring. As a result they will tend to avoid smaller projects because the associated information costs prohibit further consideration. Although the threshold varies from one provider to another, it would be sensible not to take offence if rejected when your project is seeking external equity funding for amounts less than one half or one million dollars.

The difficulty of obtaining venture funding is illustrated with the following humorous story:

> *An entrepreneurship student ready to launch a company asked his business professor, "How do you get money to start a company?"*
>
> *The professor replied, "There are two ways, the regular way and the miraculous way."*
>
> *The budding entrepreneur begged, "Please explain this to me."*
>
> *The professor responded, "The regular way is for you to pray, then the heavens part and the angels come down and give you the money."*
>
> *A look of surprise came over the student's face. "Well, Professor, what then is the miraculous way?"*
>
> *The professor answered, "The miraculous way is when a venture capitalist gives you the money."*

2. **Business angels**—A more informal source of external equity funding may be available from "business angels." These are high net-worth individuals who want to invest in new and exciting business prospects. The criteria that a particular business angel applies to evaluate projects may differ from institutional venture capitalists and also from other angels. Although the risk/reward calculation is still critical in the decision-making process, there are other more personal factors that may drive the decision as to whether to consider a project and then get involved financially. Many business angels have their own experience of successful entrepreneurship they wish to apply to the benefit of new ventures. They may also wish to get closely involved in the operation of those ventures. As a result of these differences in motivation, the business angel may be prepared to invest significant amounts of time and money to assess a potential prospect. The return sought may involve less tangible elements such as personal satisfaction in addition to financial returns.

3. **Government grants**—An additional source of effective external equity provision is in the form of government grants at a regional, state or national level. These are usually designed to encourage particular kinds of business development in terms of the sectors or localities in which they operate. Such grants may not be conditional on the sharing of business ownership but represent external equity in the sense that they constitute risk capital with no recourse to repayment in the event of failure. Entrepreneurs should check the availability of such grants at an appropriate source such as regional development agencies or the small business administration at **www.sba.gov** (or **www.nesta.uk** in Great Britain) for further information.

Assistance may also be available from regional government or private groups in the form of "enterprise zones" or business incubators, where no-cost or low-cost office space is provided to the entrepreneur for a limited startup period, possibly coupled with tax incentives.

But for the vast majority of startup businesses, external equity funding is not a realistic option. The amounts sought will either be too small for venture capitalists, insufficiently interesting for business angel participation, and non-qualifying for government grants. In this case, entrepreneurs who need external finance must consider going into debt.

Financing through loans

The evaluation and monitoring costs associated with external equity financing also influence an entrepreneur's access to borrowing. By far the most popular sources of debt finance for entrepreneurs and businesses are banks (and to a lesser degree credit unions and mortgage brokers). Although loans from family and friends are extremely important, they should often be treated as external equity finance since those involved may not have a high expectation of repayment but may want to participate at least to some small degree in the business.

To understand how banks approach the assessment of loan applications, it is helpful to consider two basic alternatives. The first refers to the "income gearing approach"; it focuses upon the profit prospects of the project for which the loan is required. The second is referred to as the "capital gearing approach"; it focuses upon the accumulated assets and credit history of entrepreneurs and their businesses.

1. **The income gearing approach**—Under this approach of assessing a loan application, bankers are primarily concerned about ensuring that the income generated by the project under consideration will be sufficient to pay back the loan with interest and money to spare. In short, they will focus upon the prospects of the business and the extent to which it is likely to succeed. Thus evaluation and monitoring require very similar information as was the case for external equity financing. It is rarely in the bank's interests to provide funding on this basis unless the amounts are relatively trivial or there is a long and close relationship between the bank and the entrepreneur.

2. **The capital gearing approach**—In order to avoid the information costs associated with an income-gearing or prospects-based approach, bankers will usually seek some form of security or collateral to set against the loan. For the

entrepreneur with a startup enterprise this may present difficulties both with business and personal collateral.

With the exception of land and buildings, reliance upon *business capital* in the form of plant and equipment may be problematic since the cost of their acquisition is not reflected in their value for collateral. The purchase price for the entrepreneur will typically be significantly higher than the collateral value to the banker because the entrepreneur will pay the market price for a productive machine whereas the banker will take a "carcass valuation" approach. For example, if a textile-based business buys a computerized knitting machine and there is a downturn in the market, which causes the business to fail, then the value of that machine, at auction, may be very low. For businesses intending to grow rapidly, this problem of business collateral valuation has particular significance since the costs of acquiring new plant and equipment massively outstrip the extent to which these can be used for security and business collateral.

Because of the valuation problems with business collateral, banks will often seek *personal collateral* from the entrepreneur to secure a business loan, such as a home. This claim over personal assets may take a variety of forms but, effectively, removes the protection provided by limited liability. This means that the bank will have first call on these assets in the event of business failure and loan default. For potential entrepreneurs, there is a more serious consequence of this approach, because if they do not have sufficient personal assets, they may not have access to bank loans—or simply put, no collateral, no loan.

Tips for gaining access to external sources of financial support
FOR VENTURE CAPITAL, entrepreneurs should:
- Prepare a very clear and persuasive business plan.
- Show in that plan an annual internal rate of return of at least 35%.
- Be prepared to share at least 30% of their business in terms of external equity participation.

FOR BUSINESS ANGELS, entrepreneurs should:
- Provide a clear business plan.
- Indicate the potential in that plan for significant annual internal rates of return often in excess of 20%.
- Be prepared to share a significant portion of the business in terms of external equity participation.

- Be prepared to involve the external investor in daily business decisions and operations.
- If the "business angel" is a family member or friend, have a formal contract—deal with them professionally as "outside investors."

FOR GOVERNMENT GRANTS AND LOAN GUARANTEES, entrepreneurs should:

- Seek advice as to the evaluation criteria that will be applied to the grant application and the monitoring activity and performance levels that will be expected when a grant is awarded.
- Expect a large amount of paperwork—most likely more than the typical inventor-entrepreneur may want to live with.
- Investigate (in the US) loan guarantees provided by SBA of up to $2 million (in 2002), and grants up to $800,000 from various government agencies through SBIR (Small Business Innovation Research).

FOR BANK LOANS, entrepreneurs should:

- Ascertain the precise information requirements that the lending agency will impose and find out why this information is required.
- Be prepared to offer regular monitoring information about the business and the project's performance in advance or in excess of bank requirements. Research has shown that a more informed and closer relationship between banks and entrepreneurs results in improved terms for the loan and more effective bank support in the event of short-term and unexpected fluctuations in trading conditions.
- Be prepared to develop a clear business plan with explicit monitoring structures for obtaining business performance information.
- Be prepared to forewarn the lending agencies of changing future financial requirements.
- Be prepared to shop around at different banks to get the best deal.

FOR ENCOURAGEMENT, entrepreneurs should:

- Remember the adage "If at first you don't succeed, try, try again." Make sure your venture is skillfully presented as sound and exciting.
- Look at the situation from the viewpoint of the funding provider. Imagine that you are asked to finance a business—what information and assurances would you require? What criteria would you want met before investing in the enterprise?
- Consider operating on a shoestring. The need for "doing more with less" has

been a powerful incentive for many entrepreneurs in starting their successful companies. Later, they felt that a large amount of available money would have been detrimental to their being lean and competitive. Too much startup funding has led to bad spending habits and the downfall of many a dot-com in the last few years.

Looking beyond startup

In Chapter 2, we briefly introduced two different types of enterprises: the small startup businesses coming from individuals mainly seeking self-employment and the entrepreneurs with a vision for taking their enterprise to the "next level" and building a significant, long-lived company (Ref. 2.5). A common goal for both types is surviving beyond startup for a good number of years. However, according to US statistics, 60 percent of businesses do not make it past the six-year mark, and only about 20 percent survive for ten years. The majority of new businesses are of the first type; they are also known as *lifestyle* enterprises since they support their owners with a satisfactory living in a location that they like. However, to survive in today's globally competitive market, all entrepreneurs need long-range, strategic thinking, and they must learn new management skills (including communication, finance, and administration) beyond the technical or sales skills they had as startup entrepreneurs.

Let's go back for a moment to Figure 1.1 and consider a product's life cycle. A typical generic curve is shown in this figure. But for a fad item, the time span can be very short (perhaps only a few months), with sales peaking very quickly and just as quickly dropping off to almost nothing. On the other hand, some products may have much shallower peak sales with an extended lifespan. Note that for all three patterns, sales and profits will eventually decline. Thus you must consider what you should do to prevent your business from declining and dying as well.

Beyond long-term strategic thinking in quadrant D, two "producer" tasks in quadrant A—quality monitoring and continuous improvement—can be used to maintain your business operating profitably at a constant or growing level.

Quality monitoring

Entrepreneurs must keep in mind that quality is not a fixed commodity. In the 1970s, consumers have learned (mostly from the Japanese) to expect quality routinely, even in low-cost products. If you do not seek to continuously improve your product, your competition will do it. Thus, you need to make plans from the start of your enterprise to monitor and improve the quality of your product and of your service. You can collect data from your customers directly and indirectly. Indirect information may not give you a complete picture. You may be able to track service complaints or product returns and warranty claims, and you may note a loss in sales over time. But what does this data tell you about repeat business or about disgruntled customers who simply disappear (taking their friends and acquaintances with them through bad word-of-mouth advertising). The result can be significant loss of market share. Thus you may need to periodically resurvey your customers and potential customers - their needs, their experiences, their perceptions (or your competition) may have changed. What improvements would they like to see in your products and in your service? A car repair business may do just as good a job as the competition down the street, but if the car owners were provided with a pager to notify them when their car is ready for pickup (while they are shopping at the nearby mall), they would most likely patronize the business that saves them time.

Because of an initial lack of competition or later fierce pressures for survival, some companies may neglect to pay attention to *total quality management*. TQM has become essential to the long-term survival of companies, and even small enterprises can benefit from applying many of the principles for managing change, anticipate future markets, and develop innovative products and services in a process of continuous improvement. When the Pugh method is used to develop a top-quality product, it will be robust or able to stand up to competition, for a while. However, when your feedback shows that your customers' expectations have changed, it is time for a new round of problem solving to come up with a substantial change and improvement in your product. TQM may need an initial investment of about one percent of your company's revenue, but this investment in quality will quickly pay back since—as shown by Genichi Taguchi—an increase in quality leads to cost reduction. The creative problem solving process can be used to implement TQM and find solutions for customer problems (Ref. 3.5).

Continuous improvement

An important advantage of continuous improvement is that it reduces the risk involved with innovation. Continuous improvement can be thought of as focused, limited, or incremental innovation and is thus much more acceptable, manageable, and likely to occur in a corporate environment which would feel threatened by unpredictable and unleashed creativity. An attitude of continuous improvement dispersed through an organization over the long run prepares the way for creative breakthroughs. Again, with a mindset that habitually uses creative thinking and effective problem solving to improve their products and services, entrepreneurs will have a significant competitive edge. Include continuous improvement and quality monitoring among your goals for long-range survival and growth in your business plan!

Writing a business plan

Much of the information that you have learned, assembled or reviewed in working through Part 2 of this book now comes together in the business plan. As you have seen above, a business plan is required if you are trying to get funding for your enterprise. A business plan can also serve to guide policies and strategies in your new business. However, and this is a very important point, a business plan is NOT the business, because no sooner have you written the plan, the conditions will change, and you must have a flexible mindset to adjust quickly and look for opportunities in change! Therefore, do not follow the plan blindly. A simple plan may have a dozen or so pages; a more comprehensive plan may be 40 or more pages long. Thus we will not include an example of a business plan here. However, we will indicate the main components of the plan and what information flows into it, and we will give you web sites where you can get useful advice on writing a business plan.

Elements of a business plan

A typical business plan has four sections: (1) front matter, (2) description of the business, (3) financial information, and (4) supporting documentation. Make sure the information is as complete as you can make it, and take care to be neat and professional and avoid using too much technical jargon and acronyms that are not defined.

Front matter

1. **Cover sheet**, including your name as the contact person, the name of the business, a logo and/or slogan, addresses and phone number.
2. **Statement of purpose**, including names of all co-owners, amounts of financing desired (if applicable), and a confidentiality statement.
3. **Table of contents**, with page numbers.

Description of the business

4. Description of the business in the format of an **executive summary**. Include a brief discussion of the industry, your competitive advantage, the planned financing, key members of your business team, and any other important information. *TIP: Although this item appears first in the main body of the plan, write it last, after you have completed all sections. It should not exceed two pages!*

5. Information on the **context of your business,** including a summary of the current state of the industry, market trends, your competitors, possible barriers to your entry, and the future trends and outlook of the industry. *If you have completed a market analysis and the exploration of the industry context, you should have the information needed to write this section. Make sure to present solid data and a realistic assessment of your competition.*

6. **Detailed description of your business,** including its legal format and the product(s) and/or services that you plan to offer. Highlight why customers will want your product. Indicate the location of the business, the competition you foresee facing, and the targeted market or customers. *The key information on your product should come from your final round of the Pugh evaluation. The information on the customers should be available from the original customer surveys as well as from the results of the marketing plan and market test (if one was conducted).*

7. **Description of your operational plan and procedures,** including—for a product—the production process, purchasing, and delivery and distribution, or—in the case of a service—the logistics of how you plan to deliver your services. Discuss how your approach compares to that of your major competitors. Also discuss the resources that are needed (and how these have been or will be acquired—including plant, offices, and equipment). Include a description of the qualifications of your personnel and your management plan and organizational structure if more than just a few people will be involved. *This information forms the implementation plan (in the producer's mindset, as described in Chapter 4). You can include a summary of your quality monitoring and continuous improvement plans here as well.*

8. **Description of your marketing plan,** including your strategic image, methods of advertising, your advertising budget, and your advertising implementation and monitoring plan—how will you analyze and gauge the success of your ad campaign? *Some of this information is available from your marketing analysis, and the monitoring plan needs to be developed now as one of the producer tasks.*

9. **Assessment of risk:** Discuss how you see the risks in view of your competition and barriers to entry, the trends and anticipated future developments, and then outline the methods you plan to use to deal with the risks. Include a description of your insurance coverage. *A risk assessment was recommended for the final solution(s) during the later stages of the Pugh evaluation. Include any late-breaking information here. Remember that any innovative enterprise carries with it a considerable amount of risk—describe how you are prepared to deal with this calculated risk.*

Financial information

You may need to enlist the help of an accountant to prepare these calculations and data sheets. The SBA web site below gives detailed instructions on how to calculate and complete the financial data sheets. Make sure that all financial data is accurate or based on realistic projections.

10. **Overview of the financial plan**: This summary is especially important if a large amount of financial data is included here for starting up a substantial enterprise.

11. Describe the **sources and uses of funding**; include loan applications if any.

12. Describe your **capital equipment** and also include a supplies list.

13. Prepare a **balance sheet** and include a discussion of assumptions for your projections.

14. Estimate your **startup costs**.

15. Prepare a **break-even analysis**.

16. Prepare **income projections** (profit and loss statements) in several formats: (a) 3-year summary; (b) first-year detail by month; (c) second and third-year detail by quarters.

17. Also prepare **cash-flow projections** in the same format as the income projections.

Supporting documentation

Here you can include tax returns of the principals for the last three years; personal financial statements (all banks have these forms); a copy of any relevant contracts (franchise, license, building leases or purchase agreements); a copy of the resumes of key personnel and principals, and copies of letters of intent from suppliers. Also include any other documents that can support your plan (i.e., a sample of your product brochure).

Web-based resources

- A useful site for business planning is the MIT Enterprise Forum at **http://web.mit.edu/entforum/www/Business_Plans/pblans.html**. This site lists many guides or handbooks on how to write a business plan.
- Easy-to-read directions and examples on writing a business plan can be found at **www.inc.com/writing_a_business_plan/index/html**.
- An interesting site for entrepreneurs is at **www.entreworld.org**.

- A web search for "business plan" will bring up many commercial sites having software on sale for writing a business plan.
- You can find further information on writing a business plan at the website, **www.sba.gov/starting** (then click on "business plan"). Table 10.4 lists available SBA web information about getting started in your business. We recommend that you review each topic to ensure you have not left out any important aspects (or resources) for starting up your enterprise.

***Table 10.4** Available SBA Web Information About Getting Started*

1.   Do I have what it takes to own/manage a small business?
2.   What business should I choose?
3.   What is a business plan and why do I need one?
4.   Why do I need to define my business in detail?
5.   What legal aspects do I need to consider?
6.   What do I need to succeed in a business?
7.   Would a partner make it easier to be successful?
8.   How can I find qualified employees?
9.   How do I set wage levels?
10.   What other financial responsibilities do I have for employees?
11.   What kind of security measures must I take?
12.   Should I hire family members to work for me?
13.   Do I need a computer?
14.   What about telecommunications?
15.   How much money do I need to get started?
16.   What are the alternatives in financing a business?
17.   What do I have to do to get a loan?
18.   What kind of profits can I expect?
19.   What should I know about accounting and bookkeeping?
20.   How do I set up the right record-keeping system?
21.   What financial statements will I need?
22.   What does marketing involve?
23.   What is my market potential?
24.   What about advertising?
25.   How do I set price levels?
26.   Are some locations better than others?
27.   Is it better to lease or buy the store (plant) & equipment?
28.   Can I operate a business from my home?
29.   How do I find out about suppliers/manufacturers/distributors?
30.   Where can I go for help?
31.   What do I do when I'm ready?
32.   All Most Asked Business Startup Questions

Checklist for business startup

This final list for "producers" getting ready to launch their enterprises includes many items that have been mentioned previously—check off all tasks that you have completed and cross out those that do not pertain to your particular planned enterprise. It is assumed that you are properly motivated, that you have determined your enterprise to be feasible, and that you have a marketable product or service.

Financial info (likely determined as part of your business plan)

___ Assess your personal financial resources.

___ Calculate your startup and operating expenses (for two years).

___ Project your revenue (for at least two years).

___ Project your cash flow (for at least two years).

___ Assess the profit potential of your business (with timeline).

___ Investigate potential sources of funding, including family, friends, equity, grants, and debt.

Research

___ Research your industry, your market niche/target, your customers, and your competition.

___ Research suitable locations and zoning laws; choose the "best" depending on your priority (lifestyle and profit expectations). Keep in mind that some localities and states (in the US) are much more business-friendly than others. Also investigate if a location in a business incubator makes sense for you.

___ Develop your business plan (including marketing).

___ Create a company and product name; check for availability; file for trademark protection and domain name. If you have not yet done so, apply for patent and copyright protection.

___ Research available free help or counseling from SBA Service Corps of Retired Executives (www.score.org) or small business development centers (www.sba.gov/SBDC/index.html).

___ Research a suitable business model that matches your thinking style profile as well as the type of business you will manage. Business management is a very broad topic that is largely outside the scope of this book on entrepreneurship. However, for your startup to be successful, you need to carefully plan how you will manage your employees, your business growth, your assets, as well as change and taking advantage of unexpected opportunities.

External relationships

___ Search out potential vendors and suppliers, as well as shipping/delivery providers if applicable.

___ Select a suitable attorney, accountant, and insurance agent.

___ Decide on legal business format; file with appropriate local, state, and federal agencies. In the US, apply for FEIN number (from the IRS) and any other state and local franchise, property, and sales tax numbers, as well as for for licenses and permits as applicable.

___ Implement your funding plan; sign legal contracts as applicable.

___ Establish a business bank account and credit card or credit line (if expedient).

___ Join appropriate business organizations such as the Chamber of Commerce, the Better Business Bureau, and trade organizations in your line of business.

___ Create an advisory board (an invaluable source of advice if chosen wisely).

___ Arrange to have the business listed in local directories (including telephone).

Infrastructure

___ Establish record-keeping procedures.

___ Decide on staffing and assign roles/responsibilities; hire and train employees as needed to meet the requirements (if not available from owners/partners). Have signed non-compete agreements to protect your trade secrets.

___ Set up operational policies and procedures.

___ Set up a monitoring system so all local codes and industry regulations will be met.

___ Order raw materials or inventory.

___ Set up a website.

___ Set an official starting date; organize appropriate media notices.

___ Put your sales/marketing plan into operation.

___ Equip your premises (purchased facility, rented space, or home office/garage), including telephone, Internet access/safeguards, and other utilities.

___ Obtain insurance as appropriate: property, fire, flood, theft, auto, liability, employee group benefits (medical/life/disability), workers' compensation, and business interruption.

!!! NOW LAUNCH YOUR ENTERPRISE !!!

What have you learned from this book?

We trust that what you learned here in this book will encourage you to start a creative enterprise. We strongly recommend that you keep notes about your process and periodically evaluate the results. As stated at the beginning of Part 2, we cannot guarantee that you will succeed in your business if you follow all the steps for effective problem solving—there are too many intangibles involved. You can, however, increase the odds. According to Jeffry Timmons (Ref. 9.1),

Having relevant experience, know-how, attitudes, behaviors, and skills appropriate for a particular venture opportunity can dramatically improve the odds for success. The other side of the coin is that if an entrepreneur does not have these, then he or she will have to learn them while launching and growing the business. The tuition for such an approach is often greater than most entrepreneurs can afford.

In the end, an entrepreneur learns by doing—like an apprentice. Many entrepreneurs experience false starts or even failures at various stages in product and business development. Yet what they learn through this process will help them to succeed in their next venture. Patience is required as a successful venture can take seven or more years before showing any capital gains.

Also, we can be encouraged from the experiences of entrepreneurs who have turned early failure into success—see *Michael Gershman, Getting It Right the Second Time* (Addison-Wesley, 1990) for stories.

Table 10.5 Examples of "Failures" that Were Turned into a Success

Success after some false starts — Henry Ford
Failed experiments and product prototypes — Thomas Edison
Difficulty of finding a "concept" buyer — Chester Carlson
No sale of invention; became manufacturer of product — James Dyson
Changed product name from SMP to Mathematica — Steve Wolfram
Changing marketing approach — Kimberly-Clark (Kleenex, Kotex)
Idea had to wait for supporting technology — Ralph Gillette
Change in product from pigs to one fish to many fish — Kenny Yap
Change in "customer" (parents to corporations) — Bright Horizons
New application, much larger market — Jim Knott, Riverdale Mills
From diversification to single focus — Applied Materials
Old technology, no job; new parter, new technology — Jim Clark
High risk ad campaigns; failures yield publicity — Richard Branson

You may want to investigate some of the examples listed in Table 10.5. Conduct a case study—try to identify the problem-solving steps and mindsets used and analyze how well each step was followed. How did these entrepreneurs use failure as a stepping-stone to success?

Keep on Moving! — a final word

Figure 10.4 shows the London Eye, the result of a design competition for a British Landmark for the millenium. It took years to obtain the required construction permits. British Airways provided financial support because they recognized the potential as a "European" tourist attraction. The wheel opened two months behind schedule due to the engineering problems, but it has now been so successful and popular that Londoners hope it will become a permanent structure like the Eiffel Tower in Paris.

There are many ways to go forward, but only one way of standing still.
FDR

KEEP ON MOVING!

Figure 10.4 *The London Eye—symbol of an innovative enterprise*   ***Photo:*** *Martin Binks*

Index